D1417241

Blazing Pencils

Other Books by Meredith Sue Willis

Fiction

A Space Apart
Higher Ground
Only Great Changes

Nonfiction

Personal Fiction Writing

Blazing Pencils

A Guide to Writing Fiction and Essays

By Meredith Sue Willis

Teachers & Writers Collaborative
New York

Funding for this publication has been provided by the National Endowment for the Arts and the New York State Council on the Arts.

Teachers & Writers Collaborative's programs also receive funding from the Aaron Diamond Foundation, Manufacturer's Hanover Trust Co., the Morgan Stanley Foundation, the New York Times Company Foundation, the Scherman Foundation, the Helena Rubinstein Foundation, and the DeWitt Wallace-Reader's Digest Fund.

Teachers & Writers Collaborative is especially grateful for the support of Mr. Bingham's Trust for Charity.

Cover art by George Schneeman
Hand motif by Chris Edgar
Printed by Philmark Lithographics, New York, NY

Teachers & Writers Collaborative
5 Union Square West
New York, NY 10003

ISBN 0-915924-19-6
Second printing

Library of Congress Cataloging-in-Publication Data

Willis, Meredith Sue.
    Blazing pencils : a guide to writing fiction and essays / by
Meredith Sue Willis.
        p.   cm.
    Includes bibliographical references.
    Summary: Introduces methods and ideas for writing fiction and non-fiction.
    ISBN 0-915924-19-6
    1. English language—Composition and exercises—Juvenile literature.
2. Fiction—Authorship—Juvenile literature.
3. Creative writing—Juvenile literature. I. Title.
LB1576.W4886   1990
808'.042—dc20   90–31084
                                                         DIP
                                                         AC

Acknowledgments

I would like to thank all the students whose work is included here, and many others whose work has given me ideas. In particular, I want to thank students and teachers at Arroyo Grande High School, Arroyo Grande, California; the High School of Creative Writing, New York, New York; Lincoln High School, Shinnston, West Virginia; Tenafly Middle School, Tenafly, New Jersey; and Watsessing School, Bloomfield, New Jersey.

Individual students who shared their time, writings, enthusiasm, and some specific ideas for assignments included Carissa Bielamowicz, Christina Dos Reis, Andrea Ferreira, Eric James, Erin Ross, Erica Schreiber, Peter Sciaino, and Tyler Shaw.

I also want to thank three teachers who tested whole chapters of this book with their English classes: Karen Morgan at Lincoln High School; George Edmondson at Arroyo Grande High School; and, also at Arroyo Grande, my sister Christine Willis, a dedicated and creative teacher to whom I dedicate this book.

—Sue Willis

The Quick Guide to This Book

One of the main points of this book is that writing fiction and writing essays aren't always that different.

If, though, you are in a hurry and want to learn *only* about writing **fiction**, read chapters 1, 3, 4, 7, and 9.

If you want to learn *only* about writing **essays**, read chapters 1, 2, 5, 6, and 8.

(But in the long run it's better if you read the whole book.)

Any time you encounter the hand symbol,

it means you should put the book aside and write.

Table of Contents

CHAPTER 1

——Where Do Ideas Come From?——
Fiction & Nonfiction

INTRODUCTION

Fiction writing and nonfiction writing start in exactly the same way—with a person remembering something, or thinking about a problem, or just sitting around feeling bored.

For example, I might be staring out the window with nothing in particular on my mind, and I see a woman in a red dress who reminds me of my grandmother. I recall the good times I used to have at my grandmother's old-fashioned country store where she sold everything from shoes and toothpaste to candy and chewing tobacco, and I might start writing down some memories about that place:

> My grandmother's store sat at a curve in the road on the back side of Wise Mountain. It was a general merchandise store and mail drop-off for all the farms and hollows on that side of the mountain. People used to come down at noon and wait for the mail. They would pull wooden boxes and nail-kegs near the iron stove, even in hot summer weather, and tell each other stories for hours and hours.

This is a type of nonfiction writing called a *place profile*. You can write a profile or portrait of a person, too, and if I had written the full story of my grandmother's life, that would have been a *biography*.

But there is more that could have started from that red dress. Instead of writing about my grandmother's personality or her store, I might start thinking about how she used to make quilts. I could do research on quilts at the library and museum, and write a research paper about quilts for school or an article for a magazine.

Then again, I might go out and interview my friends about their grandmothers and write a composition that compares different types of grandmothers. Maybe my friend Edgar's grandmother is the same age as mine, but dresses like a model and owns a boutique. And maybe Suzanne's grandmother, who doesn't speak English, tells wonderful stories about life in Italy. If I decided that one type of grandmother (probably mine!) was better than all the other kinds, and I gave my reasons, I would be writing an opinion essay.

Another possibility would be to start with the grandmother or the store or the quilt or the red dress, and let my mind go and make up a story. I could write about a woman similar to my grandmother and then invent some things that happened to her. I actually wrote a short story that began this way. In my story, there is a grandmother like mine, who owns a country store and lives alone. Some men, who she thinks are escaped prisoners, come to her door.

> She. . . stood in the dark kitchen, peering at the shape on the steps, pressing at her outer door. No friendly voice saying, Hey, Mrs. Morgan. Nothing she could recognize as a Robinson or an Otis. The television was still going in the background, shooting cowboys. She made out another man down on the ground at the bottom of the steps, and at a little distance, by the garage wall, a cigarette ash glowing. Three of them, she thought, and that was when her blood ran cold. Three men, and she was sure they were convicts.[1]*

In real life, my grandmother once told us that some men escaped from a prison near where she lived, but she never claimed they came to her house. She just talked about how scared she was. For my story, I did a sort of "Let's pretend" and imagined what might have happened.

Just letting your mind drift can lead you in a lot of different writing directions. Some of the directions might lead you to write stories, and other directions might lead you to write essays. This book

* All footnotes are in the back of the book.

was written to help you wander into good ideas for fiction and nonfiction.

If you flip back a couple of pages and look at the table of contents, you'll see that the chapters about writing fiction are mixed in with the chapters about writing nonfiction. I did it this way because I don't think fiction and nonfiction are all that different. For example, that nonfictional portrait of my grandmother's actual store is part of my fictional story about the grandmother I made up.

Descriptive writing is the same whether you are writing about something real or something made up. Both fiction and nonfiction writing also use narration, action description, and dialogue. Writing about something real can give you an idea for something made-up, and vice versa. You might write a story and then decide to write an opinion essay on the same subject. A made-up story can have as much (or more) truth about real life as a nonfiction piece.

Each chapter in this book has suggestions for getting ideas and then ways of taking these raw ideas and cooking them. If you do at least one writing assignment from each of the nonfiction chapters (chapters 2, 5, 7, and 8), you will complete this book with four compositions suitable for school. If you do all of the "Seven Steps to a Story" suggestions in the fiction chapters (chapters 3, 4, 7, and 9), you will end up with a fairly long short story. Yes, that's right, in only seven easy lessons! If, on the other hand, you're the kind of person who doesn't like following instructions too closely, each chapter has other ideas to get you started on your own.

Very important: whenever you see this hand symbol

it means you should close the book and write.

Many of the assignments in this book were suggested by students. Sometimes they didn't even know they were suggesting assignments—they just did what they wanted to instead of what I told them to do, and I thought, "Hey, that's even better than *my* idea, I can try *that* with some other classes." Students who read parts of this book while I was writing it gave me even more ideas.

You might find yourself at the end of this book with a stack of beginnings that don't seem to go anywhere. There is nothing wrong with such fragments. I have drawers full of them. Every once in a while, I go back to them and finally finish something. Chapter 9 in this book has a special section on ways to get yourself to finish something. But old fragments can give you new ideas too. Or, they can just be fragments. Everything doesn't have to be finished.

Each chapter concludes with a section called "Looking Again." It's about looking back at your work or revising by making your piece longer, giving it suspense or surprise, adding an interesting lead, and making sure it tells enough but not too much.

COLLECTING IDEAS

First we need the raw materials. Where do we get our ideas for writing? Where do we get ideas for anything? The man who invented the essay, Michel de Montaigne, said he started with himself. Another way of saying this is that writers get their ideas from everywhere. You get your ideas from assignments teachers give you, from books and movies and television, from things you observe on the street or at the beach or at home or at the mall. You use your memory too—experiences you've had as recently as this morning, as long ago as when you were a baby.

It's good to collect your ideas for writing. People collect statues of elephants and banners of athletic teams. When we were very little, my sister and I used to collect sheets of toilet paper from different bathrooms we visited. Why not collect writing ideas? Some people keep a little notebook in their pocket to write in. Others write on scraps of paper and store them in a box or envelope. I use what I call an "idea journal," but it really doesn't matter what you call it, as long as it is a place to write. It could simply be a part of your regular diary, if you keep one, though some people like their personal diary to be more private.

You are welcome to use the writing notebook provided with this book for your idea journal. You could also go to the stationery section of some store and pick out a notebook to write in. Some people like little compact books: I have always liked big unlined sheets so I can draw pictures if I feel like it. But one way or the other:

• Get something to write in. Sit down with it in front of you, with a kitchen timer or stop watch or other clock. Choose a period of, say, ten minutes, and write *anything* that comes into your mind. Don't write too fast, but do write steadily, repeating a word or phrase, if you have to, rather than stopping. This is called *freewriting*.

(Remember: the hand symbol means it's time to write.)

• When the time is up, read over what you wrote. Underline the sentence or phrase or word that interests you the most (it doesn't have to be the "best written," it just has to attract your attention). Skip some lines in the idea journal and copy the part that caught your attention. Now, starting with that phrase or word or sentence, write again for another seven minutes (or whatever amount of time you choose). This is called a *directed freewriting*. The rules are the same as in freewriting. Write steadily, without stopping, and if your mind drifts from what you began with, go where your mind wants to go.

• Try freewriting and directed freewriting several times, or—even better—on several different days. Try it at different times of day and in different places (outdoors; in a public park; in a parked car).

THE MAN WHO INVENTED THE ESSAY

The man who invented the essay was called Michel (French for Michael) de Montaigne (of the Mountain). Michel de Montaigne lived about four hundred years ago (1533-1592) in a violent time when people killed each other viciously and brutally over religious differences. To get away from the violence, Montaigne moved to his house in the country. He began to write what he called *essais* (French for "something I'm trying out"). He wrote about any subject that caught his attention, but he always started with himself.

• Write a self-portrait. Try to be reasonably honest, but don't dump on yourself. Include your physical appearance and what you are good at and not so good at. Tell something about qualities you have that aren't obvious to someone looking at you. For example, you might look to the world like a normal boy who likes to be with his friends, while you have another side, *inside*, that likes to be alone to think about things in your own private way. Here is a little bit of what Montaigne said about himself:

> Now, I am a little under middle height.... In dancing, tennis, or wrestling I have been able to acquire only very slight and ordinary ability; in swimming, fencing, vaulting, and jumping, none at all. My hands are so clumsy that I cannot even write legibly enough for myself.... I do not read much better.... I cannot properly fold up a letter, nor could I ever cut a pen, nor carve at table worth a hang, nor saddle a horse, nor carry a bird correctly and let it fly, nor talk to dogs, birds, or horses.[2]

Example:

I am a short, stocky, not-so-imposing person. I have brown hair, brown eyes, or hazel, depending on what they want. Your first impression of me would probably be that I am a generally nice person, though my friends know that I get into some mischief. I am plump, and I have always been that way. I have a weird body—too fat for regular, too thin for husky, and I can't wear jeans because of my thick legs. I am an avid soccer player, though I am not gifted with the game. I have no special talents, I cannot draw, paint, or play an instrument. I can sing somewhat, though I do not feel it to be my heart's calling, and can read music somewhat. I am quite bright, and while I may be somewhat slow in the getting of something, I can immediately use it. I am agreeable, have no vices or bad habits, and am happy.
—Tyler Shaw, 8th grade

• Montaigne used to like to set himself a topic, as in a directed freewrite. You might like to try one of his topics, but if you do, don't get concerned with whether or not your writing makes sense or stays on the topic. Some of my best writing happens when I leave my subject and realize that what I started to write wasn't nearly as interesting as what I switched to. Here are some of Montaigne's topics:

Of sadness
Of idleness
Of sleep
Of fear
Of cannibals
Of smells
How we cry and laugh for the same things

Of drunkenness
Of cruelty
Of thumbs
Of anger
Of a monstrous child
Cowardice, mother of cruelty
Of presumption
Man is no better than the animals.

- Try writing about one of these topics each day for a week.

- Make up a list of your own.

- You might turn your list into cards for assignments of the sort teachers keep in a box in the classroom. You could exchange "assignments" with a friend and see which ones inspire the best writing.

OTHER IDEAS

- There are many other kinds of journals or diaries besides the writer's idea journal and the personal diary. Try a:

Commonplace book—You write down sayings and passages from your reading that appeal to you. You might include lines from songs, things you heard on television, etc.

Scrapbook—This includes news clippings, matchbooks, etc. that represent events in your life, along with writing.

Sketchbook—Instead of writing in a journal, draw what you saw or what happened to you.

Dream Book—Write your dreams every morning.

• Read the diaries of famous people (Queen Victoria) and diaries that made their writers famous (Anne Frank). Take a look too at some of the diary-like writing from the distant past—by people like Jonathan Swift or Samuel Pepys. You can even read the work of eleventh-century Japanese court ladies Murasaki Shikibu and Sei Shonagon.

• Here is the diary entry of a young girl many years ago who had recently moved to New York from Spain:

> I brought my diary to school so that I could write a few words. We are reciting geography but I can't follow it. I am going to describe the classroom, that place that I detest. The classroom is a large square room with gray woodwork, a glass door, and on the right, a big cloak closet with red curtains. After hanging up my coat and hat, I go to the 4th yellow desk in the 3rd row. Before that, when I come in, I say, Good Morning Miss Bring. I get out a pencil, a pen, an eraser and a ruler. I take a book and study. The teacher goes bing on her bell, we stand up and say a prayer made up of an Our Father, Glory to God, Hail Mary, and the blessing of the day. After that we recite the catechism, then geography, then we do arithmetic until noon. At 1 school starts again. We do dictation, composition, reading, and grammar. At 3 it's finished. There are 24 boys, 12 girls in our class. The teacher is stern, but not mean, but there are many unfair things because she has a favorite who is the meanest girl in the class and accuses everyone else very unfairly. The teacher is watching me, so I have to close my notebook.
> —Anaïs Nin[3]

• Try writing a special lunch hour journal at school, or one that you keep on the school bus, or in some other place where you go regularly.

LOOKING AGAIN

All professional writers look back at their work and make changes (revisions).

• If you have a suggestion for a change or an addition to this book —like a particularly good assignment you made up and would like to share—please send it to me, Sue Willis, c/o Teachers & Writers Collaborative at the address given on the copyright page of this book.

Now you have a journal for notes and raw ideas, and—if you have chosen to do the assignments as you read—some entries in the journal. The next chapter will suggest ways of collecting and using descriptive writing.

CHAPTER 2

————Places and People————
Nonfiction

PLACES

I remember the first thing I ever wrote. I made it up, but it seemed totally real to me. Actually, there wasn't much writing in it because it was a comic book. I could write only two words, *hi* and *hay*, but I meant *hey* the way you say *hey* to your friend instead of hay for horses. My comic book was very exciting to me. The characters were fighting and riding horses and falling off a very dangerous cliff.

I showed it to my father, who was probably busy doing something else, and he said, "That's nice, but why do the people say 'Hay' and 'Hi'?" I realized that he *didn't even know about the cliff.* He wasn't getting any of the story, any of the excitement that was in my mind. For the first time I understood that when you are writing, you have to find words to let the reader know what is in your mind.

One of the best ways to do this is through sense details. The reason the senses work so well in writing is that most of us can see, hear, smell, taste, and touch. Even people lacking one or two senses have the other ones.

If I tell you I saw a beautiful car, for example, you might or might not believe me. If we are best friends and we have talked for hours about cars, you might go along with my opinion. But if I am a stranger—if I am older than you, or from a different part of the country—how can I make you know what I mean by beautiful? I do it with sense details. I tell you the car is bright lipstick red with metallic flakes in it, and it has chrome wheels and a tiny black racing stripe, and when you sit in it, the smell of leather fills your nose, and you hear the powerful roar of the engine.

You may or may not agree with me that it is a beautiful car, but at least we know what we're talking about. I have begun to put what I experienced into words that mean something to you. That's *communication*.

• Close your eyes and slowly, in your imagination, recreate a place you have been. Imagine yourself there. Start with sounds. Is it noisy there? Is there music? Are people talking? Do you hear birds? Is there a sound of water? In your imagination, take a deep breath and breathe in the air of the place. What odors does it have? Can you smell something cooking? Is there something to taste? In your imagination, feel the air of the place. Is there a breeze? Is it hot or cold? Touch some things with your fingers: are there soft things, hard, feathery? Finally, in your imagination, look around the place. Use your senses to explore the place as long as you want.

• In your idea journal, or on a piece of paper, write as much as you can of what you experienced with your eyes closed. Try to get all five senses in, but don't worry if there's no sense of taste. Tell it however you'd like ("In my place. . ." or "I looked around me. . ." or "First I heard the sound of. . ." or whatever). Make it as long or short as you'd like, and get in as many different sense impressions as you can.

Example

The dunes were covered by a quilt of brilliant white snow that had fallen the night before. Sticking up from beneath it were a few clumps of tall, thin grass. They trembled violently in the wind, but remained standing because of the bolstering snow. The snow crunched under my feet as I walked down the dune, and a few flakes clung tenaciously to my socks. . .the sea lashed at the beach like a hungry lion. Foam-capped, greenish-grey waves threw themselves at the shore and then trailed slowly back to the sea.

I stopped and faced the ocean. Eagerly, I breathed in the sharp, salty odor of the ocean. As a wave crashed against the sand with a sound of muffled thunder, a spray of seawater hit my face and covered my lips with bitter-tasting salt.

A lone sea gull was soaring gracefully in the soft blue sky, his high-pitched flute-like calls piercing the air.

I turned back to the dunes and again climbed to the top of them. Once there, I took a final glimpse at the scene, and then ran back to the welcoming lights of the house.

—Carissa Bielamowicz, 8th grade

• Do a couple of these places, perhaps one ordinary place, one special place or one you really hate. Each time, though, start by closing your eyes and imagining yourself in the place.

• Write a sense description of a place where you used to live, or of the first time you visited a new place.

Example

I opened the door to our family's old apartment. I looked around. It was empty, nothing but the air, no toys on the floor, no furniture or boxes, no nothing. I went to my old room. I looked around my room. There were no posters of TV stars or piles of stuffed animals. There were just two little cactus plants I'd left for the new people who were going to move into the apartment. I listened real hard. Besides the traffic and the honking and yelling people, all was quiet. My mom wasn't complaining about anything because there wasn't anything to complain about, no toys on the floor or dishes to be done. I couldn't go to sleep because there was no furniture or beds. There were only blank white walls. I felt very, very bad. I was moving from the city I loved so much.

—Amy Reiter, 6th grade

- Try taking your idea journal or a little notepad to a real place—a park bench, a lounge chair in your back yard, a table in a restaurant, or on a bus or train. This time, instead of closing your eyes and imagining, observe what is actually around you, using each of your senses in turn.

- Write descriptions of five different places on five different days. Use any of the ideas above (closing your eyes, going to a real place, one you like, one you hate, etc.). Try places like a restaurant, a student hang-out, a church, a synagogue, a museum, a park, the beach, the town garbage dump, your favorite movie theater, your friend's room, the school gymnasium or playing field, a sports arena, etc. The place doesn't matter—what matters is using your senses to write about it.

You can make your place description longer by writing it as a *portrait*. You do this by adding more about it, information as well as sense impressions. I often do this kind of writing in a letter to a friend—especially if I have just visited a new place and want my friend to have some idea of what it was like. There is a whole type of article that does this in travel magazines and travel sections of newspapers. Explorers and other travelers sometimes write whole books to describe their experience of places.

Here is a place description from a book that started out as letters from a man in prison to his lawyer. The writer is trying to give a person who has never been in jail an idea of what it is like:

Usually, by the time I finish my calisthenics, the trustee (we call him tiertender, or keyman) comes by and fills my little bucket with hot water. We don't have hot running water ourselves. Each cell has a small sink with a cold-water tap, a bed, a locker, a shelf or two along the wall, and a commode. The trustee has a big bucket, with a long spout like the ones people use to water their flowers, only without the sprinkler. He pokes the spout through the bars and pours you about a gallon of hot water. My cell door doesn't have bars on it; it is a solid slab of steel with fifty-eight holes in it about the size of a half dollar, and a slot in the center, at eye level, about an inch wide and five inches long. The trustee sticks the spout through one of the little holes and pours my hot water, and in the evenings the guard slides my mail in to me through the slot. Through the same slot the convicts pass newspapers, books, candy, and cigarettes to one another.

—Eldridge Cleaver [4]

• Try writing a portrait of a place.

PEOPLE

Just as your senses fill you with an impression of a place, so do they give you information about people. Everytime you meet a new person—or even see your best friend—your senses are alert. Does the person have a new perfume or aftershave? Is he wearing a fancy new sports watch? Is her voice hoarse with a cold? When you meet someone for the first time, what is the first thing you notice? Something you see, probably. Perhaps age or sex? Is this person smiling?

I happen to be short for an adult, and one of the first things I notice is whether or not the person is taller or shorter than I am.

Clothes are an obvious thing we notice, because we make a lot of guesses about what people are like from the way they dress. We aren't always right, but it doesn't stop us from guessing. For example, what if you meet a woman dressed all in black with a cross around her neck? Don't you already think she is a nun? What about a woman wearing a gray business suit carrying a leather briefcase as she waits for the bus or a train? What do you guess is her profession? How about a young man in his late teens or early twenties, wearing all black like the woman we think is a nun—but he is wearing black leather pants and jacket with a motorcycle chain for a belt and lots of studs and spikes on his leather wrist band? Does he belong to a motorcycle club? A heavy metal rock group?

Colors give us clues (we think) about people's personalities. Someone wearing all bright colors like a garden in summer makes a different impression from someone who wears earth colors like brown, clay red, and sand. The same person, of course, might wear palm trees and flamingoes one day and a dark jacket and tie on another day. Is the person stylish or old-fashioned looking? What do you think of a person the age of your parents who dresses like a high school student?

But that is only the most obvious thing we get from just one sense, our sense of sight. What do you hear when people speak? Suppose you answer the phone at home. Can you tell if the person calling is a man or a woman? Maybe not every time, but often. Can you guess at the person's age? Mood? How about what country they come from, or what part of this country? Think of teachers you know. Do some of them shout? Do others speak very softly? Do you know anyone who loses his or her temper a lot and screams? People have speaking styles, just as they have clothing styles. Some use slang or curse and others talk a lot or a little. What is your style? What style do you like?

We think even less about using our sense of touch and sense of smell when we meet people, but we do that too—some people, for example, wear tons of cologne or perfume. You can often recognize people who smoke without ever seeing their cigarettes. After certain meals (a plate of spaghetti with garlic and oil) we sometimes take a breath freshener. If you know any little babies, you have probably noticed how some people like to nuzzle them and say how sweet and powdery they smell—and then scrunch up their noses and hand the baby back to its father and say, "Hmmm, I think somebody needs his diaper changed!" I remember being around five years old and a little chubby, and people used to squeeze my legs (I hated it!) and say, "Isn't she solid?" Do you pat your friends on the back? Shake hands? Do people in your family kiss a lot? I remember meeting my boyfriend's uncle, who was a former football player and *very large*, and he grabbed me and gave me a big hug and an enormous wet, sloppy kiss on the cheek. I got a little too much of the sense of touch with him.

• Close your eyes, as you did when thinking about a place, and think of a person you know. It is probably better to choose someone you don't know well—even someone you've only glimpsed on the street—than the person closest to you, but anyone will do. In your imagination, make yourself invisible so that you can go very close and look at the person in great detail. Touch them (remember, they can't feel it) and see if their hair is soft, if the palms of their hands have calluses. Take a whiff to check for suntan lotion or cologne or pipe tobacco. Have them speak, and notice the tone of their voice, their accent, their mood. Spend as long as you'd like in your imagination observing this person.

• Now write the sense description of the person. Use as many senses as you can.

Example

> When I look at my neighbor, I see a greasy white shirt, brown eyes, work shoes (which are very old), oil-stained jeans, brown-black hair, and white socks. A greasy-oily smell fills the air when I walk near him. The closer I get, I see that he hasn't brushed his teeth this morning. With his right arm all rough, and his left arm slick with oil, I can tell he is a man who loves doing work and especially fixing cars. Even though he is a little rude, his rough voice makes him a nice guy to me.
> —Jeff Helman, 6th grade

• Go to a public place and write your observations of the people you see there. Don't forget to notice things like their shoes and how they walk.

Example

The man I saw was a Spanish man. He was walking down the street with his head shoved into his shoulders and his arms were slapped against his sides like he was handcuffed. His 10-year-old shoes had holes in them and there were no laces. He didn't have socks on. His shirt was very dirty but not torn. It was checkered. His pants were the same and there was a grease spot on his left knee. He had glasses on so I couldn't see his eyes. His mouth had two teeth on the bottom, both on the sides. He didn't have any top teeth. He was talking to himself in Spanish. His hair was a brownish gray that was dirty and smelled disgusting. His mouth smelled like rotten anchovies. I went over and touched his hairy arm. It felt greasy and tough. He had a gray mustache with something brown in it. He looked about 45 and was a homeless, jobless, moneyless, foodless person.
—Andrew Singer, 6th grade

• Try contrasting descriptions: describe a person who appears to be rich and one who appears to be poor, and then an old person and a little baby. Don't forget to use your senses.

PROFILES OF PEOPLE

A profile of a person, like one of a place, is longer than a description, and it has more kinds of information. To write a profile of a person, you might add things about his or her personality or accomplishments. The profile explains why the person is important. Sometimes it is of a person who sets a good example—someone people might want to be like.

Example

"I know which of you like scary stories," Jackie Torrence told the kids as they sat slack-jawed in wonder. "I could tell just by looking at you." Just by looking at Jackie Torrence, 44, you can tell that she loves stories too. She does not so much sit as perch on a seat in front of her audience, leaving her body free for constant motion— her arms circling, hands fluttering, face rearranging itself into 1,000 masks. "On any given moment, on any given subject, I can tell you a story," she tells me. "I have a friend who traveled with me for 30 days. She said, 'Am I going to be bored?' I thought, 'I'll fix you.' I said, 'I want you to write down the names of the stories that I tell.' We travelled 30 days. I averaged three places a day, three stories at each place. I didn't tell the same story twice." For about 270 days a year, Torrence leaves her home in Granite Quarry, N.C., to tell her stories to school children in Washington, to visitors at folk festivals in Tennessee and even to grown-ups at New York's Lincoln Center. Some people call her the Story Lady. One of some 2,000 professional story tellers in the country, she is among the most successful.
—Michael Ryan[5]

• Write a profile of some public figure or movie or rock star you like, using your own impressions and knowledge to explain why that person is important.

• Write the profile of someone who is a bad example—it doesn't have to be a criminal maybe only your little brother or big sister.

• Write the profile of someone you know who isn't a celebrity, but who you think is interesting. A few years ago I wrote about a student of mine. He wasn't famous then or now, as far as I know, but he was a very good actor. Here is part of the profile:

The girls had trouble choosing a boy to be the prince in the Cinderella play. The boys in the class seemed either too small and delicate or else so big and mean they would destroy the magic. In the end they chose Luis, a boy who could have been the lead girl's twin. He was just her same height with the same expressive forehead and rich dark hair. Luis hadn't had a part in the boys' play earlier in the year, and he wasn't sure he liked being the only boy in the girls' play. They bullied him pretty badly too, shoving him and whispering things that I couldn't catch. One day when my back was turned, the evil stepmother kicked him in the crotch. I saw Luis pucker up struggling with tears and announce he was quitting the play. The girl playing Cinderella was mad at everyone, including me, for not stopping the incident. She certainly had no sympathy for Luis, who was as much a prop to her as the special ball gown or the slipper he fits on her foot.

Luis waited for me in the hall outside, and I only had to beg a few minutes before he reconsidered. After that I watched the tough girls more closely, making them leave the room for the more tender scenes. I was impressed with Luis: he never cracked up in giggles and spoiled takes. In the final performance, the prince and Cinderella seemed like sweet children in a dream.[6]

Example

The City Streets of New York City, where every kind of person lurks. Rich, poor, skinny, fat, young or old. The wind was blowing as I pranced down the street. Glancing to the side of me, I saw an oldish man who was carrying or pushing a shopping cart. I tried to see what he was doing. He seemed to be reaching into garbage cans and pulling out soda cans and putting them in his shopping cart. Maybe he was going to return them to the store for money. I looked again to realize he was dressed rather shabbily. A smushed old-looking hat hid most of his brown stringy hair that was sort of dangling in his face, which looked unshaved. He was wearing a brown holey coat covering his clothes. Gloves that showed his finger tops covered the rest of his hand. You could see a glimpse of black pants which ended a little before the ankle. His black shoes were dusty and resembled those of a clown, big and lopsided. You could tell he hadn't showered lately because his body odor was extremely strong and unavoidable. He was poor and it was pretty obvious. I can't tell what kind of things he liked because he was just wearing clothes and mumbling to himself. It sounded like "nablabla" from a distance. Who knows who he is or what he's doing now?

—Emily Jaffe, 6th grade

OTHER THINGS TO DO

• With a couple of friends, make a collection of portraits, perhaps of students in your home room or teachers or store keepers in your neighborhood.

Here is the beginning of a collection of profiles of teachers.

She has a soft voice. It is like a summer wind blowing softly. Her clothes are serious yet casual. She likes different colors in her clothing. Her hair is put up very nicely. She wears make-up yet looks plain. She walks like a breeze in springtime. Her hair is blondish and is up in a loose flare of style. She wears high heels but she walks as though she is barefoot in an open field of grass, walking slowly, but surely. She is a nice person, and she is serious about her work, a typewriter teacher.
—Johan Almgrer, 6th grade

I approached the man during his work, as a gym teacher.
He was wearing the Indiana University 1988 NCAA Championship Basketball Team shirt. The one I crave. He had a whistle against his chest, which was practically made out of iron, and he had a key chain with two keys dangling out of the pocket that belonged to the Nike sweatpants. He wore Converse Con low-tops and Ocean Pacific socks. His hair was a rug, and his voice bellowed whenever he said a word, which was usually an order. The man is an athlete. That was obvious from his wardrobe, and he meant business, his voice gave that away. His hideous smelling sweat made you look twice, and his glaring, brown eyes intimidated you. But, under all that, personally, he's a great guy (and a Knick fan, of course).
—Mark Levine, 6th grade

• "Take a portrait" of a friend. Don't give the name, but see if other people can recognize whom you are describing, as in a riddle. This used to be a popular game among writers in France. Gertrude Stein, an American writer who lived in Paris, wrote this one to describe the artist Picasso:

One whom some were certainly following was one who was completely charming. One whom some were certainly following was one who was charming. One whom some were following was one who was completely charming. One whom some were following was one who was certainly completely charming. . . .[7]

Would you have guessed that was about Picasso? I completely certainly wouldn't have completely, not certainly.

• Get out a magazine on a topic that interests you and read about a well-known person in the field. Look at the pictures. Now close the magazine and write everything you remember. This isn't stealing, because even if you decided to use this for a school report, all you would have to do is give the name and issue of the magazine and say you got ideas from it.

• Cut out pictures of the person (or place) and make a collage (different words and pictures cut out and pasted together in a way you like) that could go along with your profile article.

LOOKING AGAIN: ADDING DETAILS

After you've done as many of the exercises in this chapter as you want, pick the one that interests you most and read it again. Then:

• Add a color to your description. Even if you already have several colors, add another. Don't just add "red" to "roses" or "blue" to "sky." Choose something in the piece that could be "colored in" (a piece of clothing, a cat, a fingernail, a car), and insert some interesting color before it. In the following piece, find the added color:

> I am in a quiet room in my uncle's vacation house in Florida. The only sound is the ceiling fan spinning faster and faster. As the fan is on longer, it starts to get cooler. Then when you turn the fan off, it is quiet. It gets warmer and warmer. The closet and floor feel soft. The walls feel harsh and rough. It is a spacious room. The room doesn't have a scent except when I start to use suntan lotions. It smells strong and has a strong effect on the scent of the room. The room is an ivory-white color and very pretty. When I'm there, I feel good and I feel like someone (my uncle) cares about me and my feelings.
> —Cathy Sofianides, 6th grade

• Cathy added something else to her piece as well as "ivory-white." She added a final sentence that summarized or gave her feelings about the place that she was describing. "When I'm there," Cathy wrote, "I feel good and I feel like someone (my uncle) cares about me and my feelings." Can you add something to your piece that shows your feelings about being there?

- Add a sound word to your piece.

Example

The moist heat lays on you like a heavy damp towel. Above, a parrot is squawking. I hear a stream bubbling and something moving in the bushes. For once in my life I am alone.
—John Hooper, 9th grade

- Look over one of the profiles of a person or place that you've written. Look for a word that you could make more specific. Usually this will be something like "big" or "beautiful" or "ugly." How do I, the reader, know exactly what you mean by those words? Try to change one of them to something more exact. Before you write, read the following by sixth-grader Dana Tunick:

My Aunt Susann lives in sunny California. She is always in style. She is medium sized and very pretty. She is skinny and wears only the most in-style clothes. She has dark red, almost amber-colored hair. She has green eyes that are like the sea after a big storm. Her skin is rough in some places but in others it's like silk. She wears perfume sometimes, and I like the perfume she wears.

For her revision, Dana decided that "in style" is not exact enough. What if you who are reading this book didn't know what was in style when Dana wrote this piece? After "she is always in style" she added:

She wears skin-tight jeans or big pants and tee shirts or big bulky sweaters. She wears push down socks and earrings. Mostly she wears sneakers and boots, but when she goes out, she wears high-heeled shoes.

Describing vividly is a way to put yourself back in a place you remember, or to bring a person you remember back into your mind.

Describing with the senses is also one of the best ways to communicate your experience to someone else.

There is a third thing this kind of describing can do: it can give you a great way to begin writing a story.

CHAPTER 3

Beginning Somewhere
Fiction

PLACES GIVE YOU IDEAS

Places and people are not only subjects for profiles, they are also two essential building blocks of fiction writing. In the last chapter I asked you to close your eyes and pretend to be in a real place using each of your five senses. You can also use your senses to imagine a place you've never been, or you can start with a real place and change it. This is one of the best ways I know to get an idea for a story.

Several of my stories and one of my novels started with places. My novel *Higher Ground* began after I took a walk in the country with my mother and aunt. They were talking as fast as their mouths would work: they used to walk here, meet their friends here, go swimming in this old creek.

"Who lived in that house?" I asked, pointing at an empty shack up on the hill. They didn't know, and while they talked, I wandered up to the house.

It was not one of your haunted mansions; it had never been much more than a shack. The porch was broken down, and I stepped over missing boards to look in the windows. There was a horribly stained sink with all the plumbing exposed, and some kind of animal had made a nest in the corner. I heard a door swinging and creaking somewhere.

I started wondering to myself: who had lived here? What would it be like to live in a place like this with no neighbors and a long walk to the main road? It reminded me of a brother and sister from out in the country that I went to high school with.

As I walked back down the hill, I started playing "What If," and I imagined that the brother and sister I used to know had lived in this house. What if, instead of only knowing them a little, I had gotten to know them well? What if I had once been with them in that very shack of a house? What would we have said, what would have happened? I observed the old house; I remembered; I made some things up. That is how I got the idea for my novel:

> Ahead of me was a weather-gray house with a porch. On one side, like crosses with their tops knocked off, were two clothes line poles. Only the roof of the barn was visible as the hill started down again.
>
> Dogs barked, and a person came out on the porch and stood in the shadows. . . .[8]

Seven Steps to a Finished Story: Step One

Get yourself in a good imagining mood. Choose a comfortable spot: your favorite chair, park bench, or the back seat of the family car on a long trip (I used to make up a lot of stories there). Close your eyes, and imagine you're in a place. This can either be a real place or a made-up one, or a place that is partly real and partly made up.

Just as in the last chapter you used all your senses to explore a real place, now use all your senses to imagine this made-up place: People talking? Birds? Music? Sound of water? Breathe in the air of the place. Cooking odors? Salt air? Garbage? Is there a breeze? Is it hot, cold? Hard and smooth? Rocks? Grass? If grass, short or tall? In your imagination use all your senses to explore the place. If your mind drifts, that is perfectly fine. When you have used all of your senses a couple of times, write down as much as you can about this place. Don't worry about order or spelling, just get down a lot of sense impressions of your place.

Example

I was on the top of a hill. It was a wide open field, with trees on both sides of me. The wind was blowing, and you could hear it whistling as it made its way through the trees. The grass was short from where it had just been mowed, and you could see the cows on the other side of the hill. . . .
—Angela Goff, 9th grade

PLACES SET A MOOD

When you start with a place like this, part of what you are doing is setting the mood for your story.

Examples

As the waves swept the shore, I could hear beautiful sea gulls and their peaceful screams. The crisp salt water air surrounded my body. And the sand felt like I was standing in cocoa. And the sun seemed as if it were lying on the surface of the sea, like a big red cherry. . . .
—Christopher Shrader, 9th grade

A planet. . . like a ball of blood. There is death in the air, children and parents slaughtered by some force. The river once clear as the air is now red as a bloody rose. . . .
—Jason Collins, 9th grade

The first author sets a calm and pleasant mood. The second author, on the other hand, isn't fooling around: violence and horror are the order of the day.

As you are reading or watching TV, you may not even be aware of how the setting gets you in the mood for what's to come. It's obvious, of course, when scary music in a movie tells you something frightening is about to happen. For example, did you ever see the movie *Jaws*, in which a giant shark kills a lot of people? Every time the shark is about to attack, there is this loud panting-pounding music, while the camera follows the innocent swimmer. Even television commercials do this to you: they show a lovely beach (no shark) with beautiful, tanned young people playing volley ball, getting pleasantly warm, and then refreshing themselves with Colossal Cola, or Pink-Sugar Flavored Fruitless Juice, or whatever. Using a place, they get you in a mood, then try to sell their product.

• Write a description of a place that sets a mood.

Example

The smell of fresh roses fills the room. I feel the warmth of a crackling orange fire. I feel elegant in my long lavender lacy dress, yet loneliness and emptiness consume me. I feel like Cinderella alone at a ball, with the soft mellow sounds of classical music. The room is silent except for the music. I can hear my soft breaths of air in my ears. It is too quiet to seem like reality. Too sad to seem like fantasy.

—Claire Rottin, 6th grade

• Read over the places you've described (or take one from chapter 2), pick one that interests you, and write again, this time adding more made-up details. Even if the description is of an empty lot that you pass every day, make up a couple of things about it. Put in a made-up tree or an abandoned flying saucer.

I am in the middle of writing a science fiction/fantasy novel, and one of the things about fantasy, of course, is that you have to invent almost everything. You can't just think back to the house you used to live in. I have to decide how many suns my world has (two) and what color they are (one is bluish and the other pink). This makes me start wondering what color that makes the sky. And how often do the suns rise and set? That is just the beginning. I have to decide on the weather (they have terrible freezing hailstorms) and plants and animals (or is it some other kind of life or no life at all?). Every time I work on this story, I add more details:

> There was a curve with an opening between rocks on one side, and a view between them. Espere stepped out, found herself on a flat boulder that overlooked the sea. She had never seen the sea, but there was no mistaking the vast thickness of mist over a flat surface that went farther than the desert. Her father had told her that you never see the surface of the sea, only the rolling blue fog that clings to it like a garment and makes all hidden, all treacherous.

• Even if you don't particularly like science fiction, try writing a paragraph describing a world that is entirely different from ours. Is it cold or hot? Are there deserts? Ocean? What lives there? Does it swim, creep, fly, bounce—or slime?

Example

> A horrid land covered with dark, thick fog. The mutants who live there are sickly grey with no eyes. They have to use their other four senses. Huge trees surround the place, the fog lives in their leaves, allowing no light to penetrate. Shrieks and screams fill the air.
> —Jonathan Southern, 9th grade

- Describe a place that would be a good setting for a mystery story.

- Write one for an adventure story or a love story.

- Try one that makes fun of the standard types of stories (mystery, science fiction, etc.).

Example

It was on the moons of Triton when I met her eyes of the purest green: all 10 of them. Green as the grass which grew under her toenail.... I loved her, so I sent her a dozen packages of toilet paper....
—Mike Crayton, 9th grade

OTHER THINGS TO DO

- Imagine and write about a place that is the ultimate wish fulfillment of a person of your age group. What is a day in that place like? Is the person who lives there happy? If not, is the person able to go back to the real world? What happens?

- Describe a place that is bad, ugly, or disgusting. After you have described it, tell a story about what happens there.

- Do the same thing with a place that is good, beautiful, and wonderful. Compare the two pieces. Is one more interesting than the other? A lot of writers find ugliness easier to describe than beauty. Is this true for you?

• Describe a place, then exchange your description with a friend who then tells what happens there. Meanwhile, you finish the one your friend started.

• Do a pass-around piece. A group of people sit in a circle. Each person has a piece of paper and writes for one minute about how a certain place *looks*. Then everyone passes to the right and reads what was written by the previous person and then writes what that place *sounds* like. Pass again, read again, adding how the place *feels*, then pass, read, and add *smells*, and finally *tastes*. Read the finished pieces aloud.

• Do the same writing game, but this time the only rule is that one description will be ugly (and everyone who adds to it has to add ugliness); one will be frightening; one beautiful; one exciting, etc. You can use whatever moods you want.

• Make a collection of magazine and newspaper pictures of places that look intriguing. Put them aside and use them if you are ever short of writing ideas.

• Read aloud and record one of the place descriptions. Pretend that you are walking through it, perhaps adding sound effects: "It was a truly magnificent waterfall...[turn on the water faucet]...Yes, listen to it splash!"

• A few days later, listen to your recording and see if you want to make any changes in the original piece. Perhaps some of the sound effects you recorded will give you an idea for sound details to add.

LOOKING AGAIN: ADDING METAPHORS

• Take one of your story settings, and add at least one metaphor (a metaphor is a description of one thing as if it were another thing— "the sky was a bar of dark chocolate") or simile (the same thing using "like" or "as" — "the lights in the pool were like eyes"). You are probably already using metaphors and similes in your writing— I would be surprised if you weren't, because we use them every day in ordinary talk. Just a few pages back, Mike Crayton wrote that a girl's eyes were "green as the grass which grew under her toenail." In Chapter 2, Carissa Bielamowicz's description of the ocean said that it lashed at the beach like a hungry lion.

Even if you already have metaphors in your story setting, add a few as a kind of enrichment, and as a way of making what you want to say even more precise. Instead of saying "It was a large room," say "The room was as large as a supermarket" or "The enormous drum of a room echoed as I walked through it." The thing that keeps people reading—and the thing that entertains the writer best too—is the part that really makes things alive: not "The room smells bad" but "The place smelled like rotten meat." Not "They called each other names," but "Joey called Eddie a pea brain," or even better, " 'Eddie my man,' sneered Joey, 'you have always been a pea brain.'"

California

Splash. The crystal clear teal-blue water of the pool shines right into my face like a light halo. The pool is warm and lighted. It stands out like electric eyes next to the dark chocolate black sky. I like it because I feel free.

—Lena Shamoun, 6th grade

• Go through one of your pieces and make a list of metaphors and similes. Can you think of some that are more interesting? Avoid saying that something is as red as a rose or as white as snow. Do you know how often those similes get used? Too often. Can you come up with something else red that is more interesting? As red as Fiesta Crimson nail polish? White like a fresh opened container of plain yoghurt? Replace the old metaphors and similes in your description with new ones.

Making a place alive and vivid with words is one way to get a story started, but it will really begin to *move* when the people come in. That's what the next chapter is about.

CHAPTER 4

People for a Story

Fiction

PEOPLE IN THE PLACE

Pretend you are sitting in a theater looking at an almost empty stage. Or, pretend you are watching a movie with a long shot of the desert and mountains. Or, you are in a church with sweet scented flowers and wedding music coming from the organ. You have looked around, listened, taken a deep breath, and then, suddenly, it happens. At the church, the flower girl leads in the wedding procession. In the movie theater, the screen shows a motorcycle and zooms in on the rider in his black leather jumpsuit. At the theater, a woman wearing a leotard and a mask runs on stage gasping.

You know that it has really begun now—the church service, the movie, the play—because the people have entered. Everything we write or watch or experience takes on life from the people in it. Even in an animal story, you get involved because the animals have personalities, just like people.

Every time I work on my science fiction novel, no matter how much time I spend on the details of the alien world where it is taking place, the story always gets more interesting to me when a character comes in. I use all the same techniques for writing about people that I use for describing places—how they look, sound, smell, feel—but more seems to happen when I describe the people:

> Big Cook was the tallest woman in the city. She would have towered well over seven feet, had her ankles been stronger, had she not stooped. She held herself up with two canes like columns. Her voice was deep and hoarse, and she smelled of cooking oil and strange spices, because she knew all there was to know about food preparation—and poisons. Big Cook lived in perpetual pain from her overloaded joints, with no family, famous in the city and generally feared, in spite of her physical disability.

Plot begins to happen when people come in: Big Cook knows a lot about poisons. Hmmm. . . .

Seven Steps to a Finished Story: Step Two

Read over the setting you wrote in chapter 3 that holds your interest best. (It might be an attractive place or an ugly one.) Close your eyes, put yourself back in that place. Just be there for a little while and then, *have someone come into the scene.* If possible, just let this happen on its own, so you are almost observing it rather than making it up. It may take a while: be patient. Someone will come.

When a person finally enters your scene, examine him or her using your senses the way you did in chapter 2. What style of clothing? How is his hair cut? Does he wear aftershave, or smoke? Make her speak, and listen for an accent: can you tell if she comes from the city or country? Does she speak quickly? Does she use many words or few? What is she talking about? How would her hair or skin feel if you touched it?

The writing assignment, of course, is to use sense details to describe the person who comes into your place. The description doesn't have to be long, and if something begins to happen—if the character begins to talk or even if someone else comes into the scene—write on! *The idea is to get a story started, not to follow instructions.*

Example

I was sitting in my room. I looked around and saw my pink and purple heart wallpaper. I also saw my bed and my dresser. I listened to the sound of Samantha Fox singing on my new radio. I smelled spaghetti sauce cooking downstairs. I felt my soft, white blanket on my bed.

As I was sitting there, Kerry Bird walked in. Kerry is a four-year-old that I babysit for. She has shoulder-length blonde hair that is almost white. I can always smell the baby shampoo in her hair. She has beautiful, big, blue eyes. She has soft, light skin.

That day she was wearing pink overalls and a white blouse. She came over and sat on my bed. She began to talk. She has a big, squeaky voice, too big for her little body. She began to tell me about what she had done in nursery school that day. She talked non-stop for fifteen minutes. Then she asked me when I would babysit again. I answered her and she asked if we could color when I came over to her house. She got ready to leave and I softly touched her face. It was so soft and cold from being outside.

—Maureen Collins, 6th grade

What do you suppose might happen next in Maureen's story? Could you imagine something unexpected and exciting? Perhaps the little girl gets into some danger and the narrator has to save her.

In the next one, the setting is ominous:

The Pushover

I am in New York and I'm walking down the street. As I'm walking, I hear footsteps but when I look, I don't see anyone. It is hard to see with all the smog.

I look around and see cigarettes burning, cars stripped to nothing. There are cans dumped all over. I look up and see smoke in the air and bullet holes in traffic lights.

I walk further and hear mice squeaking, garbage cans clinking, and winds gusting. I turn the corner and hear a rather deep voice say, "Hey kid, got a dime?" I keep walking and I pass the bum. He says, "I asked you a question." I keep walking, and he grabs my shoulder with his cold hand. I am up close and smell dry whiskey under his breath. I say, "Got change of a twenty?" He says, "No, give me that." I say, "No." He holds me. With my other hand, I search my pockets and find a half dollar. I give him that. I run, but before that, I push his rough face to knock him down. He doesn't fall, so I blow at him and then he falls. While I am running, I think to myself, "He was a pushover."
—Robert Doriety, 6th grade

• Write another scene to continue either Maureen or Robert's story.

The Pushover (Continued)

...As I ventured on down the drab sidewalk I noticed the local girls were still working that night. It's funny they come and go almost faster than I can blink. After venturing farther, I'm approached by a sleazy clown dressed in enough gold to start a mine. I can see he is doped out severely and has "the stuff around his nostrils." Suddenly he pulls out a switchblade! Motionless, I stare, I question my own senses as I stare in awe. I tell myself, Run! Run! Are you stupid he'll kill you! At last, I burst out a forceful blow to his head. And people always said I was stupid for carrying a brick. I run into a deserted alley to escape. At last I am safe, I sit down and relax. Then, as if my day wasn't horrible enough, I hear large bellowing sounds from the trash compactor beside me. Oh! That horrible screeching, piercing sound. It almost sounds like a cat being stepped on. Then, it stops! Silence. . . . . . .CLANG!!!! It crashes out. My heart is in my throat. What could it be? A cat. I feel really stupid, as I sit and pet the "horrible beast." I laugh. How could I have been so stupid?
—Don Jersey, 11th grade

• If it hasn't already happened, bring a second person into your story. Add another (briefer) description, and then see what happens between the two people.

• Try bringing in a *third* person that the other two have never met or even seen before; or, let it be someone that one of them knows but the other doesn't.

As you write these sense details describing your characters, notice whether or not you are writing about someone you like. We ordinarily think that we prefer the most beautiful and attractive person, but in real life, it's often the other way around. We come to like, say, the smell of a certain pipe tobacco, because someone we loved used to smoke that brand. The opposite is true too: that stunningly handsome boy with the wonderful muscles and perfect tan might have a smile with something unpleasant in it. As you write, be aware of how you feel about the person you are writing about (your feelings might change as you write), and try to *show* through your description how you feel.

How do you think this writer feels about the character?

> Alice, tall like a man, with soft woolly hair spread out in tangles like a feathered hat and her face oily and her legs ashy, whose beauty I never quite believed because she valued it so little but was real. Real like wild flowers and uncut grass, real like the knotty sky-reach of a dead tree. Beauty of warm brown eyes in a round dark face and of teeth somehow always white and clean and of lips moist and open, out of which rolled the voice and the laughter, deep and breathless, rolling out the strong and secret beauty of her soul.
>
> Alice of the streets. Gentle walking on long legs. Close-kneed. Careful. Stopping sometimes at our house on her way to unknown places and other people. She came wearing loose flowered dresses and she sat in our chairs rubbing her too-big knees that sometimes hurt, and we gathered, Momma, my sisters and I, to hear the beautiful bad-woman talk and feel the rolling laughter, always sure that she left more than she came for. I accepted the tender touch of her hands on my hair or my face or my arms like favors I never returned. I clung to the sounds of her words and the light of her smiles like stolen fruit.
>
> —Paulette Childress White[9]

• Describe a character you love or admire who isn't pretty or handsome in the usual way.

• Describe a character twice. First, pretend you don't like the character (but don't say so directly). Then describe the same character again, but pretend you do like him or her. Remember, you aren't allowed just to tell how you feel about the character, you have to show it. Don't *tell* that "Bernie was a jerk and a dufus." *Show* it. Lots of books about fiction writing will give you that as a handy rule: "Show, don't tell." You might have Bernie dress a certain way, but it would be much better to show what a jerk he is by some things he says or does.

ACTION WRITING

Most of the people in these assignments have been standing still for their portraits, but it is important to put them in action, too. To show that Bernie is a stupidhead, you will want him to do something funny or awful or disgusting. Describe how he runs or what he does with his hands. How people move shows a lot about them. A young man might look boastful from the way he rolls his body from side to side as he walks. Some diseases even give their victims a characteristic way of walking—people with Parkinson's disease take tiny steps and carry their heads far forward. Someone nervous (perhaps they are walking alone on a dark street at night) might glance behind them frequently.

• Think of a person in a certain mood. It could be one of the characters in your story, but doesn't have to be. Show how this person is feeling through a gesture. Is he feeling angry? What does he do with his hands? Is he nervous? Does he chew his lips? Rub his nose? Bounce from one foot to the other?

Example

As we walked into the room we could see Josh was in a bad mood.
He sat at his desk quietly, showing no emotion. His arms were
crossed and his head was nodding forward a little bit. His eyes were
looking straight at the floor and his eyebrows were sloped towards
his nose. Every once in a while his leg would move up and down
and shake him and his chair. After seeing Josh, we decided to leave
him alone. . . .
—Patrick Moore, 11th grade

• Do the same thing, but describe a person who is in one mood
(say, sad) and then in another mood (say, cheerful). How do they
walk in one mood? How do they walk in the other?

Example

Depression settled about her shoulders like a cloud. Her eyes were
not shining any longer, and her mouth dropped slightly at the corners in a half-frown. Her step was slow, as if she was carrying a great
burden too heavy for her to bear. She lowered herself to the over-
stuffed chair, crossing her legs Indian-style and holding a pillow to
her chest. She made a stark and lonely figure as she sat there alone,
thinking her private thoughts and speaking to no one. Every once
in a while, she would hug the pillow tightly to her as though drawing comfort from a warm embrace.
—Terri Hoops, 11th grade

You can show even more about what a character is like, or what
the character is feeling, by describing his or her movements and
gestures. What happens when this character whom you have shown
to be angry (jaw thrust forward, hands in fists) decides to throw
a punch? You can simply say, "And then Sally slapped Frank's face.
Frank punched Sally. Sally gave Frank a karate chop and won the

fight." Do you remember, though, how disappointed I was when I was a little kid and my father didn't get the story I was writing because my words didn't communicate the excitement? You may be able to see this thing with Frank and Sally vividly in your mind: it may even be funny. There might be groans, moans, blood, but the way I wrote it above doesn't get any of that across—no sounds, no excitement, no humor.

• After a sports event or dance, or even after watching some little kids play on the playground, try to write *in as much detail as possible* exactly what they did. How was José standing as he swung for his big triple in the bottom of the ninth? Was there a special sound as the bat hit the ball? Can you describe a dance so well that I could imitate it from your words?

If you are writing about José's triple, don't let the reader know till the end that it was a good hit. Tell how he stood, maybe the expression on his face, his nervous habit of rubbing his nose with the back of his hand, or the way his shoulders looked like they were going to split his shirt as he took the swing—then the crack of the bat, and the outcome.

Some of the hardest actions to describe are the most ordinary ones. These actions are tricky to describe because, on the one hand, you want to see very clearly in your mind what is happening so it isn't confusing, but on the other hand, you don't want to write it in so much detail that someone reading it goes to sleep. How would you describe to someone a man eating a slice of pizza? (You could make it funny.) Two girls fighting in the school yard?

In my science fiction novel, I have been writing some fight scenes and other action. I find myself closing my eyes often to make a movie screen in my mind and try to picture what exactly is going on. Then I write everything I see, and later try to shorten it:

She saw three human men wearing metal and leather. They made as little sound as possible, and pulled back their javelins, making no move to parley, attacking, three at once, from three directions.

This is the lethal attack, Espere thought in a strange sort of calm. She moved quickly, as her father had taught her, so that a boulder partially protected her body, and a javelin struck the rock where she had been standing.

They did not see her flying dragon. Perhaps they never thought to look up. It brushed their dragon off balance and plunged directly for the men, slashed one of them across the chest. The man cried out, and as he fell, released his javelin into the air, and it struck his own dragon.

Simultaneous with the razor slash, the dragon struck a second man with the horny forward joint of one wing and threw its body sideways, catching the third man with its belly hooks. Two of the men were running away: she could hear them scrambling in the rocks. The enemy dragon was grounded, dragging a wing where a javelin pricked out. Flopping, trying to get airborne.

But her dragon had leapt to the top of a boulder, spread its wings, and now dropped down again, at the fallen man, caught his arm between its mandibles, snapped, and the arm was separate from the man.

• Try a piece of action writing of something exciting: climbing a cliff, a daring rescue, a battle scene, a race. Try to make it very clear: pretend you are watching it on a movie screen in your mind.

Example

But the trouble just began. A couple of his bum buddies jumped out in front of me from behind two old rusted garbage dumpsters. One wore an old raincoat which resembled a shower curtain, and the other wore an old ragged jumpsuit with a knife in his hand. They started pushing me backwards into the doorway of an old steam house. They both had knives which probably couldn't cut hot butter, but I wasn't about to find out. One swung the knife at me. I ducked and gave him a right directly into his stomach. The other wrapped

his arm around my neck and tried to cut my throat. Luckily he missed my throat and cut his arm. He began to bleed instantly. He fled in panic along with the other one. So I finished my journey home, peeking around every corner and garbage can. I got into my house, sat down, and felt something on my neck. It was warm blood from my throat. I ran to the phone to call the hospital, but the phone was dead. Suddenly the lights went out and everything was silent. I thought to myself, "It's going to be a long night."
—David Weaver, 11th grade

• Now try writing about something ordinary: cleaning teeth, climbing into bed, bouncing a rubber ball. What can you do to make it interesting? Have it turn funny? ("Now she slowly lifts the red plastic brush near, slowly parts her lips, brings the brush closer, closer! Contact! Yes, ladies and gentlemen, there is toothpaste on her teeth!")

OTHER THINGS TO DO

• Go out for a walk and "take a snapshot in words" of a real person's actions. Describe that person moving or working or talking.

• Make up a background and personality for the character.

• Use a picture from a magazine. Write the description of the character, adding anything you want.

• Make up an exaggerated person—that is, if the character you are describing is skinny, make them incredibly skinny. This sketch was written a long time ago, and some of the words aren't spelled quite the way we would spell them:

He would have measured above six feet in height had he stood upright; but he stooped very much; was very narrow in the shoulders ....As for his thighs, they were long and slender, like those of a grasshopper; his face was, at least, half a yard in length, brown and shrivelled, with projecting cheekbones, little grey eyes on the greenish hue, a large hook-nose, a pointed chin, a mouth from ear to ear, very ill furnished with teeth, and a high, narrow fore-head, well furrowed with wrinkles. His horse was exactly in the stile of its rider; a resurrection of dry bones which (as we afterwards learned) he valued exceedingly, as the only present he had ever received in his life.

—Tobias Smollett [10]

• Write how one of the characters you have described would introduce himself or herself.

• Take one of your friend's descriptions and act out the character, complete with walk, tone of voice, special gestures, etc.

• With two other people, play the game where one does an action while the second is out of the room. Then a third friend (or as many as are around) describes the action on paper. They read it back to the person who was outside, the object being to see if the descriptions are precise enough for the person who was out to do the same action. It's a lot harder than it sounds.

LOOKING AGAIN: CUTTING DETAILS

• Read the following description of a person and see how many words you can cut, saving only the most interesting details:

Mack was a really big strong, muscular guy, as muscular as a professional wrestler. He had huge muscles in his chest and enormous, strong, powerful biceps. He flexed his big strong biceps whenever he had the chance. He liked to show off how strong, muscular, and powerful he was. He was especially proud of his hulklike, magnificently muscular biceps. He stood about six foot four inches, and weighed nearly three hundred pounds, but it was all big, heavy, strong muscle. He was as strong as a really big and powerful ox.

• Take one of your own descriptions and see if you can remove three adjectives. Does this help your piece or make it worse?

• Try cutting any five words of your choice. Is this better or worse?

• Do the same thing for someone else's piece while they do it for yours. Do you like the results better? If not, change it back.

• In this day and age, people tend to get bored with description. A hundred years ago, writers would go on for pages and pages describing. This was partly because people had *seen* less. For example, a person might never have seen a tiger and would be interested in a long description of what it looks like, whereas today almost any little kid recognizes a tiger from television, pictures, books, or a trip to the zoo. How would you modernize the description of the skinny man by Tobias Smollett? Or do you like it the way it is?

• Read the beginning of the story below and continue it as if it were your own. That means you can do absolutely anything you want to it! Add to it, cut, or change whatever you want.

The room had a yellow wall with posters hanging up. It was bright. I felt my soft, pink pillow while I was listening to my sister's stereo. I just then caught the smell of the cookies my grandmother had taken out of the oven. I could just taste the gooey chocolate chips that were as big as dimes.

My sister walked in and said, "Hi," in a soft, unusual voice. I got up and touched her hair. The front was soft and curled back. The back of her hair was up in a bun. Her face was smooth. I took her hands in mine. They felt rough. I saw her dressed in clothes I have never seen before. She was dressed in a long red skirt that came just below her knees. There was a thick red belt connecting a white lace shirt. She had on red stockings with white spots on them. She was wearing white shoes with heels and red bows on the front. She looked almost like a business woman.

—Dawn Geraci, 6th grade

• Here is an excerpt from a story called "Irita Mullins" that I wrote when I was in high school. It describes Irita, the main character. The one telling the story is her teacher.

Irita must have been about fourteen at the time—the oldest living Mullins child—but she already towered well above my five feet five inches, and she was built like a goddess. Her hair was a long, violently black mass and she had extremely heavy but well-shaped eyebrows; they half hid her bright eyes.

She carried herself, there in the midst of those lice-infested, dirt-encrusted vermin, like a queen. She wore a grey feed sack rag, much too small for her, yet she could have been wearing ermine, so proud and dignified she was. I compared her in my mind to what a Valkyrie should look like.

What would you do to make this description better?

In fiction and nonfiction alike, we use sense details to make the reader experience what we experienced. The next two chapters, both nonfiction, will be about other ways to get things across to a reader—first various kinds of facts and information, then stories from real life. After that we'll go back to fiction again, but we'll still be telling stories and communicating information.

CHAPTER 5

WRITING TO GIVE INFORMATION

Nonfiction

EVERYTHING YOU WRITE IS INFORMATION

One of the main things writing is supposed to do is communicate. Actually, there is a lot more to communication than writing and talking. In the last chapter, for example, I talked about how much is communicated by the type of clothing people wear, by the sound of their voices, by how they smell. Sometimes, what I want to communicate is information about how I feel: if I write a letter to a company because the bicycle I bought from them fell apart the first time I got on it, then I am communicating how angry I am. I am also communicating that they had better send me another bicycle. Part of the last chapter was specifically about how to communicate information about action. Even doing freewriting in your idea journal is a way of writing information about what was going on in your mind.

RESEARCH

Are you aware that you can write an informative paper using only what is in your mind, without ever leaving your own room or even your bed?

• 1. Think of two things—soccer/swimming; a hard teacher/an easy teacher; being an older brother versus being a younger one; your two best friends and how they differ; two types of pets. Make a list of how they are alike and how they are different. These lists are your information—just the same as if you'd made a list of information from magazines in a library or an encyclopedia.

2. Next, think of an interesting beginning, maybe like the one below, about the difference between people who make a big mess in their rooms and those who are extremely neat:

> There are two kinds of people in the world—those who have a horror of a vacuum and those with a horror of the things that fill it. . . .*[11]

3. After you have your opening, write (in sentences) your other ideas of ways in which the two things are alike, ways they are different. You can either write a whole paragraph about your very strict teacher and then a whole paragraph about your easy teacher, or you can say all the good things about both in one paragraph and all the bad things in another paragraph.

---

* By *vacuum* she means "empty space," not "vacuum cleaner."

Example

Baseball and basketball are both team sports, but baseball is a little different. Eighteen people play baseball at one time, but the action is only focused on one person at a time, and the action performed by each player has a bigger consequence in the game. For example, the pitcher pitches the ball, the batter hits the ball, and a fielder catches the ball. Only 3 of 18 people are involved....
—Eric James, 9th grade

4. Finally, find a conclusion that ties it all together: "And the truth must be told. Our possessions possess us."[12]

• You might also try some information gathering or research outside of your head. You still don't have to go to the library, or even out of your own home. Look for something you can find a lot of in your house: back copies of *Mad* magazine? Several different products of a single kind—how many soaps do you have? Cereal boxes? Types of soda? Whatever the thing you've decided to research, write a card for each issue or item, or give them a page in your idea journal, and write down descriptions, quotations, or even—if you are of the experimental type—taste each one or try it out. In any case, make notes on your little cards.

For the writing, work just as you did for the comparison essay:

1. An introduction.

2. A paragraph about each thing or product, describing the characteristics you observed.

3. A conclusion. If it was a matter of tasting cola drinks, you may want to let yourself go here and really praise your favorite.

- If you find you like doing this, try a slightly bigger project. Perhaps you'll do interviews, and base your information on what people tell you. If you do this, be sure to give credit to the person you are quoting. Suppose you write an article on "Youth Looks at the Opposite Sex." If you quote "Girlfriends are a dime a dozen," you could credit the speaker in a footnote, or you could credit the speaker in the body of the article itself: "'I've never met a boy you could trust," says fourteen-year-old Joanie Pauley.

- Try a group project in which you (or several of you together) start with interviews, but also get a couple of books or magazines with articles on the same topic (Teen spending? Hairstyles? Should skateboarding be allowed in parks? What is the best age for students to get jobs?) so that you have quotations from books and magazines as well as from live people. Ask a librarian for help if you're not sure where to look for information.

ARTICLES THAT GIVE INFORMATION ABOUT HOW TO DO SOMETHING

Another type of information article is the one that gives instructions or describes how something is done. Just as in writing a story you have to describe the action, in a "how-to" or "process" article you either describe the action or actually give instructions on how to perform it. You find instructions for any toy that has to be put together, on packets of seeds to be planted. Recipes are nothing but instructions, and so are the introductions to the standardized tests you will be taking for more years than you may care to think about.

- Choose one of the forms listed above (recipe, assemblage instructions, seed packet, tests) or any other and write a funny version or parody.

How to Kiss

1. First give a small kiss.
2. Then another, but a better one.
3. Then you really go into action.
4. Don't go wild.
5. Kiss very gently.
6. Then try to make the kiss very comfortable and long.
7. And make sure that the person likes your kiss!
   —Anonymous, 7th grade

Here are some instructions for teachers!

How to Look Busy during a Prep

1. First, always have plenty of papers on your desk. Do not keep them in an orderly fashion because it will be too easy to expose you. It is a good idea to keep a variety of papers. . .compositions, books, and folders.
2. Sit behind your desk.
3. Keep one of the side drawers open. Should someone walk in, you could simply reach into the drawer as if you were looking for something.
4. Hold a piece of paper (preferably students' work) in one hand. You could always make believe you are filing this paper in one of your many folders.
5. Sit back and relax.
6. Ignore the above and leave your room. Walk around the building. You can always say you are looking for a student, class, or teacher.
   —Anonymous Teacher, Junior High

- Now try some instructions for something you might actually teach someone to do. This could be a craft, an activity like dancing or skating, a sport, or anything else. The main point, though, is to break it down into its smallest parts, the way instructions in a recipe do.

How to Shoot a Basketball

First, hold your right hand behind the ball. Then put your left hand on the side of the ball, then you stay looking at the rim, the back of it, and you aim for it. You put the ball in any comfortable way you want to shoot, then flick your hand to push a little so the ball can go in.

—Marcos Magnus, 7th grade

- Write a recipe for a dish you or someone in your family makes from memory. Perhaps it is a special way of grilling something, perhaps it is your family's secret fried chicken recipe. Be sure to note the sorts of utensils and pans that are required, how hot the stove should be, how long to cook, any "secret" spices, etc.

Your instructions should be simple and clear. Don't stop in the middle of the recipe to tell about the time your father dropped all the tomatoes down in the coals where they turned black and inedible.

In a *process essay*, however, you could put in something funny or some extra thought. A process essay isn't instructions, but a longer essay that tells how something is done. The reason for writing it may be simply to convey how a thing is done, but it may also be to show that something is wonderful or not so good, or to suggest how it might be improved. In the following description of how something is done, Irma Velasquez remembers how her mother makes tortillas, but she is also telling how much she loves her mother.

> When the dough is kneaded, my mother digs regreased fingers into the dull white mass, tearing away smaller portions. She holds these portions in her hand, thumb upward, constricting her fingers so small balls of dough, one by one, squeeze through at the top of her fist. She rolls the balls between her palms, rounding them and dropping them back into her pan with little fleshy slaps. Over and over her hands repeat this maneuver, deftly, quickly, in a meter as unerring as that of a concert hall metronome, until the great mass of dough has been transformed into two or three dozen small balls. My mother works seemingly without ever having to look.... Smoothly turning to the stove, my mother neatly spreads the raw tortilla, with naked fingers, on her heated griddle... and soon browned tortillas, soft and steaming, lie cooling on a snowy white dish towel.[13]

• Go somewhere and quietly observe someone at work: a pizza baker, a traffic cop. Focusing in detail on movement and gesture, write down in a notebook what he or she does.

• Write a piece to show how bad something is. If, for example, you don't like some rule in your school or town, write an essay describing it in detail, and showing, by how it works, what is wrong with it.

• Sometimes fiction writing requires research too. For my science fiction novel, I wanted the people from earth to be unable to digest the plants and animals on the planet where they now live. I found an article in a medical magazine about the building blocks of our cells (DNA) that gave me a way this could be true.

Starting with some scientific fact that interests you (maybe about how in zero-gravity your muscles start to weaken?), write a short story showing how that fact could affect people (maybe an astronaut comes back to earth feeling weak and can't fight off an attacker.)

REPORTING

We get a lot of information about current events from newspaper reports. A newspaper report is a particular way of telling a true story that concentrates on getting across the main facts concisely, but without omitting anything important. Reporting style is essentially the same, whether the report is about a civil war or a pig that won the blue ribbon at the county fair. One of the well-known tricks of the news writing trade is to begin a report with the 5 W's: Who, When, What, Where, and Why.

• In your idea journal, write a "news report" on something that happened to you this very day. If it has been a dull, hot morning in midsummer with nothing to do, pretend *that* is what you have to report on, including how you finally got so incredibly bored you picked up this book on writing and started trying out some of the exercises in it.

13-Year-Old Spills Soda!

South Orange, New Jersey. It happened at 311 Prospect Street, South Orange, in the dining room of Sue Willis. Peter Sciaino, 13, was speaking to Sue Willis when suddenly a medium-sized drinking glass mysteriously collapsed onto the young man and Ms. Willis's wooden floor. The young Sciaino had no comment on the disaster at first, but later said, "It could be the most terrifying thing that has ever happened in my life." Witness Eric James was too distraught and said, "Young Peter was quite brave the way he handled it." The glass will be examined by the Essex County and South Orange police. Sue Willis was later questioned about the incident: "I have never been involved in such an accident. I am just glad my young son was not a witness to it." Peter Sciaino will seek mental help after such a traumatic experience, and Sue Willis will clean her floor and table cloth. As for the clothes of Sciaino, they will be washed by Mommy.

—Peter Sciaino, 9th grade

• Make a little newspaper. Choose something convenient to report on: the doings of your family, friends, or pets, or a report on the games played by the various teams at your school. In each case, write approximately one hundred words per report, starting with the basic facts. Notice the style that Peter Sciaino uses above to make his report sound like a news story.

Feature articles in a newspaper often begin with the 5 W's too, or most of the 5 W's. A feature article is longer than a news article and, like a profile of a person or place, has more background and description. Here is the beginning of a feature article:

Rachel Simmons, tall, 22, black, waits for a subway. The platform is nearly deserted except for a middle-aged white man leaning against a post. The man looks tired, his horn-rimmed glasses slipping down his nose. He is perhaps a clerk of some kind, wears a shirt with four ball-point pens in the pocket, a tie, a pair of worn slacks, crepe-soled shoes. Rachel doesn't pay much attention to him until two punks saunter quietly down the grimy steps onto the platform. They're in baggy pants and T-shirts, sneakers; one has on a loose leather vest with deep pockets. Rachel, though she works as a receptionist in an ad agency, can spot their thing in a second, knows for certain what's in the pockets.

The two of them pivot, check out the platform, see her and gauge her for a few seconds, then settle on the scene. They move casually behind the white man, walk past him, laughing a little too loud, eyeing the curvature of the tunnel. Then they stop, turn and head back toward the man just as nonchalantly as before, as if they're enjoying themselves. Rachel takes it all in. She heads for them just as they pull the knife. The white man is startled. One of the punks shoves him. He drops his newspaper. "Gimme the wallet." It is quick and scary, the knife a glint of steel in the low light of the tunnel. Then Rachel moves, strides quickly for them.

She yells, "Get the hell out! You're just continuing the stereotype!" She spits out the syllables, advancing on them with her height, her flashing eyes. They are taken aback. They withdraw, try to summon up some reserves, show the knife. She keeps coming, mad as hell now. "Just a part of the stereotype, fools!" she scolds.

"Shee," one of them groans, now wary of the noise, the time elapsed, looking at Rachel and heading for the exit. "We just robbin' the man." She lifts her purse, and they take off, up and out of the tunnel. The man slumps against the steel post, hugging it, not sure of what has happened.

Rachel turns, smiles, towers over him and says softly, "You're all right."[14]

This article goes ahead to talk about Rachel and how she feels about people like the punks who tried to mug the man in the subway. It spends many pages explaining why, but is still a report.

• Clip a news article or feature article from your paper. This could be from the sports page or the regular news, or even from the weather. Check to see if they use the five W's, or, anyhow, four of them. Now, as an experiment, see if you can rewrite the report from a more personal point of view. If it is a sports report about someone hitting, say, a grand slam, pretend you were the batter. Tell what was on your mind when you actually knew the ball was out of the park.

Example

My name has been announced. I'm running towards my teammates and in front of a large crowd. This is my last game and an important one. My hands are shivering. I am trying to relax, but I can't. I never performed in front of so many people. What if my

opponent makes me look bad? What if I don't perform the way I could? But what if I score more than I'm capable of? I'll go higher in the draft. What if I get hurt and it endangers my career? Should I stay safe and not play the game? But I can't do that, not to the school, not to my teammates, not to myself.
—Eddie Hidalgo, 9th grade

Sometimes this kind of reporting, which makes a story out of the facts, is called New Journalism. Here is an example of New Journalism from a book called *The Right Stuff*, which gives information about what it is like when fighter planes come in for a landing on an aircraft carrier:

> The carrier was so steady that it seemed, from up there in the air, to be resting on pilings, and the candidate usually made his first carrier landing successfully, with relief and even *élan**. Many young candidates looked like terrific aviators up to that very point—and it was not until they were actually standing on the carrier deck that they first began to wonder if they had the proper stuff, after all . . . . [The deck of the aircraft carrier] *heaved*, it moved up and down, it rolled to port (this great beast *rolled*!). . . and there were no railings whatsoever. This was a *skillet*!—a frying pan!—a short-order grill!—not gray but black, smeared with skid marks from one end to the other glistening with pools of hydraulic fluid and the occasional jet-fuel slick. . . as little men in screaming red and yellow and purple and green shirts with black Mickey Mouse helmets over their ears skittered about on the surface as if for their very lives. . . .
> —Tom Wolfe[15]

In the next chapter, we'll do more on writing about real events as if they were stories.

OTHER THINGS TO DO

• Take a serious article out of a newspaper, say one where drug dealers are arrested, and write a funny version or parody. An example would be to have two little kids selling lemonade get arrested.

* *Elan* is a French word meaning something like "pizzazz." If you do something with élan, you do it enthusiastically, with a lot of style.

59

• Make up some real or silly instructions and have someone try acting them out as you read aloud. Does this give you any ideas for changing the instructions?

• Sit down with a tape recorder and turn on the TV, but turn off the sound. If a sports event is on, play the role of the sports commentator. Write up the high points from your tape recording. Or, do the same thing with a situation comedy or movie, and write the story you made up by watching without the sound.

LOOKING AGAIN: LEADS

What is the best way to begin a piece of writing? After you've written something, and when you're ready to show it to someone else, you'll want to think about what opening line will catch the reader's attention best. I usually write my beginnings last—after I really know what my essay or story is about. Then I can go back and see how best to interest someone else in it.

Here are good ways of leading in to an essay:

• 1. Start with a question. For example: "Who killed Christopher Robin? This is the question readers of *Winnie-the-Pooh* have been asking themselves ever since the terrible fate of. . . ."

2. Start with a story. Everyone loves a story. Sometimes even the most difficult pieces of writing will begin with the story of someone in action, something happening. The subway story of Rachel and the muggers is an example of this—the whole story of the muggers is a lead to catch your interest so you'll go ahead and read the rest of the article with statistics and other, harder ideas.

• Choose one of your information papers and write three possible beginnings for it. Read just the beginnings to several friends or family members and note which one is most likely to make them read on. Do children like one lead best? Do adults prefer a different one? How about people your own age? Which age group are you writing for? Would you consider writing two different versions, for readers of different ages?

Are you really writing for your teacher? For your Uncle Zhores? For your best friend? What if no one likes the first sentence you like? Are you writing for other people, or yourself? Sometimes there is no right answer. Maybe your piece is very personal and you don't want anyone to read it except yourself. On the other hand, if you have decided to turn it in as your weekly composition for English class, then you should probably pay attention to what a teacher would find most appropriate.

One of the most interesting kinds of information we can share with other people is true experiences—reports from our own lives. That is the subject of the next chapter.

CHAPTER 6

──TRUE-LIFE NARRATIVES──
Nonfiction

PERSONAL NARRATIVE

One of the best beginnings to any nonfiction article is a little story
or anecdote. It catches people's attention; everyone likes stories.
I doubt a day goes by that you don't tell your friend a story about
something that happened to you. Some people believe that you have
to tell the story of a bad dream to a friend or else you'll have bad
luck—the dream might even come true.

• Write one of your dreams as a story.

Example

   One night I had a dream that I was walking with my aunt and
uncle and the little girl I babysit a lot. My aunt and uncle went
ahead of me and the little girl I babysit. This elderly man walked
up to us and tried to take the little girl away from me. I picked her
up and tried to run away, but he grabbed me. I tried to kick him,
but I couldn't. I also tried screaming, but I had lost my voice. My
aunt and uncle did not seem to notice me struggling. The surround-
ing area was very familiar to me. It was right down the street from
my house. I do not know how the dream ended. I woke up to the
sound of my alarm.
   —Bethany Spoo, 9th grade

Personal narratives are also about funny things that happen, like when you tell someone about going to the amusement park and how you spilled mustard all over your favorite tee shirt, or how your little cousin got lost and then, when she was found, insisted that *she* wasn't the one who got lost, it was the rest of you. Or when you describe the best play of a ball game you saw, or when your grandfather tells you about life when *he* was a boy—all of these things are personal or real-life narratives.

STORIES THAT TEACH

One reason people tell stories is to make a point: your grandfather, for example, may think kids today (like you) don't work hard enough, so he tells you about getting up before dawn to do his paper route, and how he then went to school, which *he* says was much harder in those days. He thinks that telling this story might get you to work harder. If you have a younger sister or brother, you might tell about the time you rode your bicycle through an intersection and were nearly hit by a car. The reason you tell this story is to teach your little sister or brother to be more careful.

• In your idea journal or on plain paper, write a short, true life story to teach someone something. This should be about a time when you learned a lesson. This can be serious ("How getting a job taught me to handle money better") or funny ("My first date; or, How not to get along with the opposite sex"). Maybe you will write about the day you learned to do some particular move on, say, your skateboard.

It was a hot summer day at the beach. The waves were very small and weak. My friends and I were extremely hot, so we suited up and headed out to the surf. It was so small that no one was out, so we surfed over by the pier. The pier sticks out in some parts farther than the others, so sometimes it is hard to catch a wave without "shooting the pier." Since the waves were so small, they were breaking right at the second diamond. It was almost impossible to take off on a wave without shooting the pier.

There were only four of us out, so we had a pier shooting contest. The pilings are only about four feet wide, so it is very difficult to go through them without hitting one of them. For the first forty-five minutes we were all successfully shooting the pier like it was nothing. One of my friends fell right after he got out of the pier and almost nailed it. If your surfboard hits the pier, it could mean total destruction.

It had been about an hour and a half, and we were getting tired. I took off on one of the biggest waves of the day and I caught a rail right in the diamond and fell head first. My board went crashing into the pier, but it wasn't hurt. As I was underwater, I thought I was going to get crunched. I hit one piling on my side, but I didn't get hurt. I was extremely lucky I didn't get hurt. So just remember, shooting the pier isn't the best thing to do, because it could cause major injuries and extensive damage to your equipment.

—Danny Robertson, 9th grade

My mother tells a story about her first day in high school and how there was this girl she thought she was going to hate who wore too much make-up and kept staring at her. Later the girl became a close friend. The point of the story was that you can't always trust your first impressions of people, and you never know who will turn out to be your friend. I have a story like that too:

The first time I went to a Writers' Conference, I met four people. One was a short guy with a beard and a big mouth. He drank beer all the time and seemed to have a chip on his shoulder. I got along with him well enough, but the guy I really liked was tall and blonde, well-built, with a Southern accent. There were two women too, one who was dark and beautiful who wore lovely shawls and jewelry, and another woman who dressed very simply and wore her hair cut like a man. In the end, the two I really made friends with were—

you guessed it—the short-haired woman and the guy with the beard and big mouth!

I guess my story has the same point as my mother's. Did you notice that my story also has descriptions of people? One of the things about writing is that even when you are writing a textbook or a newspaper article, you have to describe and tell stories.

• Write a story that someone in your family likes to tell over and over again.

Example

My mom told me something that once happened to her when she was younger; it's not real exciting or anything, but it's something that happened.

She said once when she was in 5th grade her family was not very wealthy by any means, and she went to school, and was eating her lunch that the school provided, and she had eaten it all, and was still hungry, so she wanted to go up for seconds. So she did. Then she ate all of her food again, and wanted to go up for thirds, so she did, and as she was walking up there, the principal stopped her and told her she could not eat lunch there anymore. So my mom started to cry, and got some mashed potatoes, and threw them in his face, and said, "Now stick that in your pipe and smoke it." He was smoking a pipe at the time.

—Priscilla Stanley, 9th grade

• Interview someone you know who is fairly old, and ask them to tell you a story about when they were young. They'll probably tell you several. Choose the one you like best and write it.

• *Make up* a story that teaches a lesson. This is a mixture of fiction and nonfiction. Fables and parables are examples of stories like this. Some of them are very old. Aesop's fables, like the one here, are at least 2,500 years old:

> Once some frogs who lived in a pond decided they would be happier if they had a king. They decided to ask Jupiter, the king of the gods, to send them one.
>
> Jupiter laughed, and for a joke threw a big log into the lake. It made such a splash that the frogs all hid. Then, when nothing happened, they came out and sat on the log and said they didn't have much respect for such a stupid king.
>
> So they asked Jupiter for another one.
>
> This time Jupiter wasn't in such a cheerful mood. He sent them a very large stork, whose favorite food was frogs. The stork stretched its long legs and plunged its long beak into the nearest frog and started to eat.
>
> The frogs sent another message to Jupiter, asking him to get rid of the frog-eating stork. This time Jupiter wasn't in a good mood at all. "Tell them," said Jupiter, "that the next time, they should let well enough alone."[16]

Actually, I've never liked that fable very much; it always seemed mean to me. I made one up about how, after all this happened, the frogs got together and had a meeting one night when the stork was asleep. In my fable, they talked about their problems and decided together to tie the stork's legs and drag it over to the river and let it float far away. The moral of my story is: The best way to make decisions is democratically.

• Read some of Aesop's fables (or others) and pick one you either like or don't like and make a modern version of it.

WRITING ANECDOTES AND MEMORIES

Sometimes we write or tell personal narratives just to share or entertain—not really expecting anyone to learn to be careful crossing streets, or to make better landings off the balance beam.

My mother had another story she used to tell about herself and her sister when they were small and lived out in the country. They had chickens in back of their house. The eggs had just hatched, and there were many little baby chickens running around fuzzy and yellow going peep peep cheep cheep. My Aunt Virginia always used to run around barefoot when she was little. One day, she jumped off a wall behind the house and landed smash! on one of these peepers. Killed it with her bare feet!

There wasn't anything in particular that my mother was trying to teach us—she still likes to go barefoot, and we never had chickens when I was a kid. It was an interesting story that made us all screw up our faces and shudder. How disgusting! What a thing to have happen!

Often, when you tell an anecdote, although you may not be trying to *teach* anyone anything—there's no moral to your story—still, you have something important to *say*.

Here is something a woman wrote about her girlhood when she was a slave in the house of a nasty woman named Mrs. Flint:

> I remember the first time I was punished. It was in the month of February. My grandmother had taken my old shoes, and replaced them with a new pair. I needed them; for several inches of snow had fallen, and it still continued to fall. When I walked through Mrs. Flint's room, their creaking grated harshly on her refined nerves. She called me to her, and asked what I had about me that made

such a horrid noise. I told her it was my new shoes. "Take them off," said she; "and if you put them on again, I'll throw them into the fire."

I took them off, and my stockings also. She then sent me a long distance, on an errand. As I went through the snow, my bare feet tingled. That night I was very hoarse; and I went to bed thinking the next day would find me sick, perhaps dead. What was my grief on waking to find myself quite well!

I had imagined if I died, or was laid up for some time, that my mistress would feel a twinge of remorse that she had so hated "the little imp," as she styled me. It was my ignorance of that mistress that gave rise to such extravagant imaginings.[17]

• Write about one of your memories. This could be something that happened when you were much younger, or it could be something that happened this morning. Tell it as a story: first this happened and then that.

Example

I was only 8 years old and in the 3rd grade when it happened. Everyone else was doing it, so I did it too. You got on the slide, and went speeding down on your feet in a squat position. It looked like a blast, until it was my turn. I started to climb up to the top of the slide. I threw a handful of sand down the slide to make it even slicker. I got on my feet, squatted down, pushed off, and sped quickly down. But before I reached the end, something happened. I fell forward and landed flat on my stomach. I also saw ½ of my front tooth ahead of me. I ran into the bathroom and looked into the mirror. I started crying hard. My front tooth was chipped. One half of it chipped off when I fell forward on the slide. I cried & cried. I called my mom & she picked me up. I finally got a bonding on it about 8 months later. This is a memory I have when I see a slide.
—Heidi Stockert, 9th grade

• Write about a memory of something either good or bad that happened to you in school. When she was about ninety years old, the famous painter Georgia O'Keeffe wrote this memory from her school days:

> The fall I was thirteen, I was taken to boarding school—a Dominican convent beyond Madison. The Sister who had charge of the art classes had beautiful large dark eyes and very white lovely hands, but she always felt a bit hot and stuffy to me. I felt like shrinking away from her.
>
> My first day in the studio she placed a white plaster cast of a baby's hand on a table, gave me some charcoal and told me to draw it. I worked laboriously—all in a cramp—drawing the baby's hand with a very heavy black line. I thought my drawing very nice and I liked doing it. When the Sister saw it she was very impatient. She said I had drawn the hand too small and my lines were all too black. She particularly emphasized the fact that it was too small. At the time I thought that she scolded me terribly. I was so embarrassed that it was difficult not to cry. The Sister sat down and drew a few light lines blocking in the way she thought the drawing should be started. It looked very strange to me—not at all beautiful like my own drawing. I wasn't convinced that she was right, but I said to myself that I would never have that happen again. I would never, never draw anything too small. So I drew the hand a little bit larger than she suggested and that whole year never made a heavy black line again. I worked mostly with a fairly hard lead pencil and always drew everything a little larger and a little lighter than I really thought it should be.[18]

• Narrate something that happened recently—maybe something funny at school or home—and pretend you are telling it to a friend.

• Write about something that took a while to happen—maybe something that changed over several months or even years.

Example

When I was thirteen years old I met this boy, Ken. He was really sweet and all, but I liked his friend, John. But every day I would go outside and play basketball with Ken. Soon our friendship grew stronger. Stronger than any other. We grew so close in half a year. Then one day he came to my house and told me he was moving, to Iowa, where his real dad lived—his parents were divorced. He was moving in one week. One week! After everything we had been together for—he was leaving me. In that one week we grew closer and closer. And when the time came for him to leave, I had to say goodbye. Saying goodbye to him was the hardest thing I've ever had to do.

I still write him and he calls me, every so often. Our love for each other was so strong, that not even thousands of miles can sever it.

—Kristen R. Copeland, 9th grade

• Describe your very earliest memory. Or several earliest memories. Can you remember anything before you could talk?

I remember that when I was about two years old, our dog died, and my mother said he had been poisoned. "Someone put ground glass in his food," she told me. She meant glass that had been ground into tiny pieces, but I always used to squat down under the bushes and look in the dirt—in the ground—for the poison glass.

—Meredith Sue Willis

• Another type of story that doesn't teach much is a joke. Write a few funny stories—not Knock-Knock jokes or one-liners, but stories that have a funny incident. The sorts of things that little kids do and say are often funny.

• Write a memory each day for five days. These might all be memories of one type like your birthdays, trips you've taken, or times you were hurt (physically or otherwise). Or you could mix them.

• Now take one of these memories, or something more recent that happened to you (a bad day at school, or the time you won or lost a game for your team?), and write this as if it were a fiction story. Stick to the facts, but try to make it dramatic and vivid. Include lots of sense details that describe the places and people. Use dialogue. Don't just say, "And then they started insulting each other." Boring. Have Justine say, "How could he like someone with as many pimples on their nose as you have?" and have Pauline answer, clenching her teeth, "At least my whole face isn't one big zit!"

You can tell it in first person, using "I said" and "I thought," or you can tell it about yourself as if you were a character: "Then Sue turned on her computer and started to write the chapter about narration."

Example

When My Best Friend Tried to Steal My Guy

One glorious and sunny day I came to school. It seemed like it was going to be a terrific day. I thought everything would be great until I turned down the hall and saw my friend hanging all over the guy I was in love with. I couldn't believe what I saw. I tried to calm down and casually walk over to them, but when I reached the twosome, the anger I was trying so hard to sustain blew up. I began yelling at her, saying, "I can never trust you. You're so twofaced! Don't you value my feelings? What are you doing?" She looked at me with red-watery eyes. While the guy I so deeply loved gazed at me in confusion (he had no idea). Then in a very soft voice, more like a whisper, she said, "I was just trying to help you. I could never do anything like that to you!" I looked at her filled with shame. I had the perplexing question in my mind, "What had I done?" Had I blown things that far out of proportion? I guess so! I collected all my pride and whole-heartedly apologized. I think I was more embarrassed than I had ever been!
—Maggie Serrano, 9th grade

WRITING LIFE STORIES

Most of the sample personal narratives in this chapter have been short. A few were part of a longer narration of someone's life, like Georgia O'Keeffe's story about her drawing lesson. Biographies (the story of a real person's life) are often written by professional writers about someone who has done a lot in life—good or bad. Autobiographies (narrations of the writer's own life), and memoirs (collections of memories that may only cover part of the author's life) don't have to be written by famous people. When people write memoirs and autobiographies, they sometimes start with their journals or diaries. Many people, both famous and not so famous, keep diaries. Several famous diaries are listed in chapter 1. You could also look again at the excerpt from "She Tells Tales for a Living" in chapter 2.

• Try writing a memoir or biography. You might do your own (including some of the memories you have already written) or the life of someone in your family (perhaps you'll interview your grandfather). You could even do your dog's. In other words, it can be long or it can be short, serious or funny. Some people even write group biographies of a family or a group of friends.

- Biographical writing does not have to tell the whole life, from beginning to end. You could only tell your memoir of, for example, the year you spent living in a different city or country. Or you could tell part of another person's life, when many changes happened to that person. Here is an example of what a teacher wrote in a report about his student, a boy who had a lot of problems:

Papo: By His Teacher

Papo came to the school last year. Sixteen years old, he couldn't read, write, or do basic math. His health was very poor: he had asthma, chronic bronchitis, and colds, and during the first part of the year, he was hospitalized several times for other health problems. Papo was convinced that he was "stupid" and couldn't learn; his frequent and prolonged absences reinforced his sense of failure and despair. Outside of school, he was involved in a lot of very negative acting out, which constantly pulled him further away from a sense of growing and achieving. Still, he finished the year at the school and, despite a great deal of hostility and paranoia, seemed to feel that he belonged here.

The first semester of this year seemed like a re-run of the last: great frustration and resistance combined with repeated absences kept him from progressing in his work although there were small changes, signs that he felt more secure. Papo smiled more often; he was less likely to provoke fights, and he studied furiously for the tests I gave. (Last year he stayed home whenever a test was scheduled.) He was in trouble because of his absences and lateness, and was on "probation" when, before Christmas, he got hepatitis and was out for six weeks. When he came back, he was a different person

—fairly regular in his attendance, very serene, and extremely serious about his work. It was a joy just to look at him. His face, which once had been tight and drawn with suspicion and anger, was sweet and peaceful. Physically, he was growing rapidly, and his once frail body was becoming strong and mature. His progress in class was extremely slow and difficult, but—for the first time—he allowed himself to be aware of and take pride in his small victories. He even participated enthusiastically in a few group activities, such as Yoga (for which he showed a remarkable natural ability), First-Aid, and Filmmaking. Papo's self-confidence had been so shattered that he could not work unless I was sitting next to him, silently reassuring him that yes, he could do it and was doing it. The beauty of the school is that, when he needed my presence, he and I were given the "luxury" of being able to work together one-on-one. Within a few months, he was spending long periods of time working on his own.

Papo was still reading on a second grade level and making steady progress when suddenly, in late April, he stopped coming to school. He had taken a full-time job working in a factory. Papo had become such a calm and steady presence in the school that we missed him a great deal, but working full-time seemed the best thing for him. He was 18 now, moving into new worlds. Whenever we saw him, he seemed very happy. Then, several months after starting the job, he lost two fingers of his right hand in an accident at the factory.

Thinking about Papo raises many unanswerable questions for me. The rage and impatience of his first year here seem so clear and understandable. What forces led to the great change in him in the middle of the year? Papo had been into some heavy stuff that could have led him to jail or worse. Why does one kid find his way through this, when so many do not? And then, after such a long and difficult struggle, why is he stopped so tragically?

Papo cannot go back to work. He has applied for disability, and says that now he will come back to the school to work on his reading. We will welcome him back, although going back to school at this time will mean, for him, being thrown back to a level he had already left behind and will raise serious conflicts for him. Hopefully we will be able to help him work them through.

This spring, after my reading class had a sensitive, spontaneous talk about the dangers of rooftops (Papo had seen a friend plunge to his death as they played there several years ago), he dictated the following thoughts: "Up on the roof, there's many things to do. You could have a lot of fun. But it's very dangerous cause you could fall off the roof. Up on the roof I like to fly birds. I like to feed them. I like to fly them. But most of all, I would like to be one of them."[19]

OTHER THINGS TO DO

• With a friend or two, make lists of one of those "First" and "Most" compositions that are often assigned in school: "My Most Embarrassing Incident," "My First Day of School," "The Worst Day of My Life." Then exchange lists of "Most" and "First" assignments and decide which assignments are best and worst. Write an assignment from your friend's list.

• Make a tape recording in which you tell one of your Mosts and Firsts. After listening to yourself *tell* the incident, try writing it and see how the written version is different from the spoken version.

• Make a collection of your and your friends' Most Embarrassing moments (or First Day at School, etc.). You might want to type the collection and/or illustrate it.

LOOKING AGAIN: MAKING IT LONGER

• Take one of the narration exercises from this chapter and make it longer by adding details the way you did in chapter 2. For example, I could take the little chickens in my mother's story and add that they were as yellow as a flock of dandelions that decided to get up and walk. Papo's teacher could have expanded the scene in which Papo lost his two fingers.

- Ask a friend to read one of your narratives. Give them a piece of paper with these questions on it, and ask for *written* answers. (This way the friend may act more like a teacher).
  1. What do you want to know more about?
  2. What needs to be explained more?

Now add to your piece what your friend needs to know. Along with *details* and *leads*, probably the most important thing to add is *things that make it clearer.*

- While revising your narrative, try some different approaches. One of the best ways to add things to a paper is to get into the fun of making the paper messy. This sounds childish, but you ought to see what this very manuscript looked like when we were adding things to it and thinking up new ideas. (See figure 1.) You probably already have ways of adding things to papers: maybe you stick things in with a little caret ($\wedge$) or an asterisk (*) or lots of long arrows.

If you haven't done it, try the scissors-and-tape method. Write the new descriptions or ideas on a separate sheet of paper and cut the original paper in two and tape the new writing where you want it to go. (See figure 2.) This makes for long, wonderfully messy sheets of paper than you can later type up or copy neatly.

This chapter has been about nonfiction stories from real life, which are a main source of fiction too. The next chapter takes us back to fiction, and how to make things happen in it.

I guess so! I collected all my pride and whole-heartedly
apologized. I think I was more embarrassed than I had ever
been!

--Maggie Serrano[49] *9th grade*

WRITING LIFE STORIES

Most of the sample personal narratives in this chapter have been
short. A few were part of a longer narration of someone's life,
like Georgia O'Keeffe's story about her drawing lesson.
Biographies (~~real life narrations of someone's~~ *the story of a real person's* life) are often
written by professional writers about someone who has done a lot in
life--good or bad. Autobiographies (narrations of ~~your own~~ *the writer's own* life),
and memoirs (collections of memories that may only cover part of
~~your~~ *the author's* life) don't have to be written by famous people. When people
write memoirs and autobiographies, they sometimes start with their
journals or diaries, ~~although not always~~. Many people, both famous
and not so famous, keep diaries. Several *(famous diaries)* are listed in Chapter 1.
You could also look again at ~~the profile of a story teller~~

antecedent unclear
people? diaries?
odd wording.

• Try writing a short ~~life story~~ *memoir or biography*. You might do your own
(including some of the memories you have already written) or the
life of someone in your family (perhaps you'll interview your
grandfather). You could even do your dog's. In other words, it

---

[49] Maggie Serrano, ~~Arroyo Grande High School, Arroyo Grande, Ca~~
~~lifornia.~~

the excerpt from "She Tells Tales for a Living" ~~on page~~ (chapter 2)

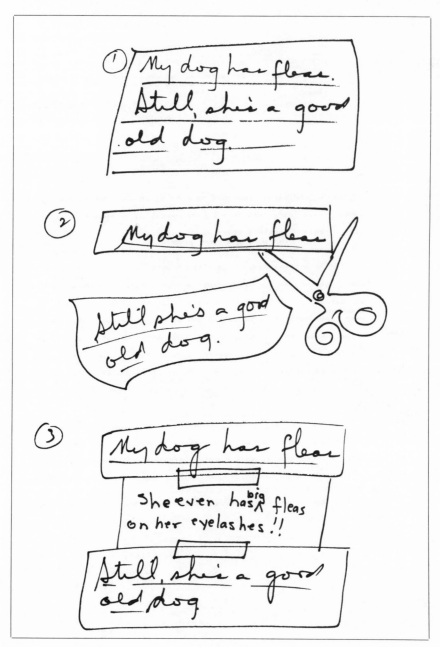

Figure 2

CHAPTER 7

———WHAT HAPPENS NEXT?———
Fiction

GETTING YOUR STORY FROM A BLANK SCREEN

When you write personal narrations like the ones in the last chapter—whether you are writing life stories or memories or anecdotes that teach a lesson—you are writing something that already happened. You might have to think hard to remember which tee shirt you ruined the day you spilled the mustard at the amusement park, or you might have to do some research by asking your grandfather to tell his story again—but the story, the events, already exist. Your job is to make something that once happened alive again.

When you write a fictional story, you may or may not have the story in your mind already. I get bored if I know too much of the story ahead of time: I like to be surprised by my own story. How, then, do you move fiction ahead? Where does the story come from? You may have already started a story in the chapters on setting and character. If you did "Seven Steps to a Finished Story: Step One and Step Two," you already have a beginning that consists of a description of a place followed by a person or some people. This is one of the best ways to start. But how do you go on? Maybe you have already figured something out; that's fine, keep writing. If you aren't sure of what to do next, try this:

Seven Steps to a Finished Story: Step Three

Read the story you've started. Close your eyes, make a blank movie screen in your head, and wait. What happens next? Does someone else enter? What do they say? Does one character walk over to the window and gaze out? Write *whatever happened when your eyes were closed*, even if it seems silly or stupid.

If you have trouble with this, try having friends do it with your piece and give their impression of what will happen next.

When you run out of ideas or energy, read what you've written again and try the movie screen once more. This works even better if you take a break before doing it again—go run around the block, or wait till tomorrow.

• Glance over what you've written (or have a friend or relative do it) and see what other facts are still needed. Is it unclear how old the people are? Is it hard to tell who hit whom in the fight? Exactly where is this weird room? Maybe you don't want these things answered, but if you do, put in a few sentences (not many!) to explain it.

• You may also need a short narration, perhaps a miniature life story—that explains how someone came to be who they are.

Please remember, though, that you may NOT want to put these things in. Plenty of good stories leave some mysteries unsolved. The most important assignment here for getting your story going is the mental movie screen where you let your mind do the work on its own.

CONFLICT

On the other hand, if you are still looking for a way to get your story moving, or moving again, try conflict.

There is almost never any story (or any life) without conflict. The science fiction novel I'm working on has conflicts between people (including actual fights where people kill each other); it has conflicts between people and nature (ice storms that can freeze you in a minute); it has conflicts within people (should the main character follow her mother's way of peace or her father's way of war?). In fact, without the conflicts, there would never have been a story. I mean, it's fine to write a cheerful postcard to your friend, but too much nice-nice gets boring. And fiction is nothing if it isn't interesting.

One of my favorite ways of seeing what happens next in a story is to add a conflict that happens in conversation or dialogue. Now a conflict does not necessarily mean a fist fight or a screaming match. Sometimes a conflict is just that one person wants something and the other person doesn't. Sometimes the conflict is that one person is trying to keep a secret. In the fantasy novel I'm writing, Espere's father and mother have a serious conflict (but with no screaming or hitting) about whether or not Espere should go on the mission for her father:

> He leaned his face forward, his scarred cheek away from Espere, his forehead and the skin over his cheekbones stretched tight, his lips like something carved out of a great boulder, and his words hissed: *"There will be no killing.* I promise you. A certain message must be delivered. Only a message, less than a message, really, a sign. One sign, and this world can ring like a bell—a single sound—"

he took a breath, he slowly turned his face from her to Espere. "I have come to ask for Espere's help."

"Mine!" In her heart, Espere had already begun to sing.

Her mother said, "I do not believe that there will be no killing. You have trained yourselves for killing, so there will be killing. Espere is not to be a part of it."

She loved her mother, but at this moment was drawn to her father. He drew her as a magnet draws things made of iron: click, snap, fastens on.

He said gently to her mother, "If you believed me, if you believed that this message would bring harmony with no killing, would you send her on this mission?"

"If I believed you," said her mother, "I would go myself."

He turned to Espere, "Do you believe me?"

She did, and she went.

Seven Steps to a Finished Story: Step Four

Add a dialogue with a conflict to your story. Do the people argue? Or is the conflict mostly inside one person? Does one person want something, while the other person is trying not to give it? Maybe it is a couple in love, and one of the people has betrayed the other. Maybe some person in authority is giving a young person a hard time.

Example

Cindy paused before she entered the elegant lobby of the St. Malicent Hotel. Checking her hands for dirt, she wiped away a bit of it on her pants. Opening the beautiful but heavy door, Cindy's attention was caught by an elegant crystal chandelier. The light from it twinkled in her eyes, and the plush white carpet on the floor buried her feet.

"Excuse me, Ma'am, may I help you?" a voice questioned.

"¿Como?" answered Cindy.

"May I help you?" the voice questioned again.

"¿Qué pasa?" Cindy answered, rather startled.

The voice was of a man dressed in red costume. He wore red boots with black trimmings and also a hat. "Whom do you wish to see?" said the man rather distastefully.

"Perdone, yo no hablo mucho inglés."

"Good Lord!" exclaimed the man. He was inspecting the girl's clothing and hair. He turned away and put his hand over his mouth. Turning back around he muttered, "Eh, who-o did you-o want-o to see-o?"

"Ey, mi tía María."

"Your what?"

"Mi tía, mi tía," she tried to explain.

"Sorry, young lady. I don't believe you belong here. I think you'd better get the hell out before I call security," threatened the man.

Sensing that he didn't want her there, she turned to leave.

"Cindy! Sweetheart, I'm sorry I'm late," said a gorgeous lady in a fox fur jacket. "¿Como está?"

"Muy bien, gracias," Cindy replied.

Looking at the doorman, Cindy's aunt said, "Carl, I see you've met my niece, Cindy."

"Yes, Ms. Lord. She is a most charming and lovely young woman," said the doorman rather stupidly.

"See you later, Carl. *Ciao!*" she exclaimed waltzing out the door, following Cindy.

--Sandra Pressley, 9th grade

• Lay the story aside for a while, then come back later the same day (or maybe a different day) and see if you can *push the scene farther.* Have the people say something else to each other. Have them do something: show if one person is nervous or angry. Perhaps give a little narration about where they go or what they do. The idea is to make it longer—and to go deeper into the characters.

• Have them talk again, later. Has something happened to one character? Having something change is one of the main points of a short story. Does one person give in to the other? Do they actually fight and does one win? Has the parent punished the child? Is the girl sorry for what she said in the previous dialogue?

Once you've found the conflict, the rest of the plot consists of figuring out how it comes out. The simplest way to finish a conflict is to have one person win. Sometimes the conflict is a hard decision that someone has to make. At the end of this book there is a story I wrote when I was a teenager in which a girl from a poor and uneducated family has to choose between her family and living with her teacher in the city. The whole story leads up to her decision.

• Write two different ways *your* conflict could be resolved. (This should just be a paragraph because it's an exercise for helping you think out the story rather than part of the story itself.)

GETTING YOUR STORY FROM A TRUE-LIFE NARRATIVE

There are lots of other ways to make a story happen. One of the most typical—the kind of thing that many fiction writers use—starts from some anecdote or personal narrative from real life. In other words, you can take anything you wrote in the previous chapter and make a story out of it by changing the ending. It isn't quite as simple as I'm making it sound, but that's the main idea.

I already talked about this a little in chapter 3 when I told about my novel *Higher Ground* that started with a place I visited with my mother and aunt, and imagined who might have lived there. There's a little more to the story of how that novel came to be. When I imagined who might have lived in that old broken-down house, I thought of a certain brother and sister I knew. In high school I had a crush on the boy, but he never knew. In *Higher Ground*, I played What If, and imagined that the boy and I did more than look at one another from across a high school auditorium.

• Try your own What If. Take any personal narrative you wrote in the last chapter. When you get to the end, *have something different happen*. In other words, if the real-life event ended with the main person embarrassed or hurt, write a new ending in which they speak up or fight back, or make it even worse, or make it funny.

A Wonderful Place

I went into a beautiful place. I felt the nice trees and bushes. I saw a lot of apples on those trees. I climbed up the tree and ate some apples. I heard beautiful noises from the birds. I jumped down from the tree. It was just an apple falling down from a tree. I saw a squirrel collecting nuts and I saw a rabbit hopping towards me. The rabbit stopped right in front of me. Then I petted the rabbit. The rabbit left. The apples looked as big as bananas. There were other fruits instead of bananas.

Then a person came next to me. He looked like a happy person. He had a southern accent and a low voice. His skin was very smooth. His body smelled clean but his breath smelled bad. He walked funny and moved his hands a lot. His hair looked like he hadn't brushed it for days. He smelled like he was going on a date with someone. I felt he would never stop talking to me. He was about an inch smaller than a tree. His eyes looked like he was worried about someone. He kept asking the same question. "Do you know anyone?" I said, "No one except you." Finally he left without saying goodbye.

—Damian Valese, 6th grade

Damian's piece comes across as rather mysterious; after you read it, you still have a lot of questions. The next step in writing your own story is to see if you need to explain some things in your story.

Who was the man in Damian's story? Why does he ask the same question? It may (or may not be) time for a little information here.

• Read over one of your personal narratives, then write a story from it changing much more than the ending. Change the main character from a girl to a boy or vice versa. If it takes place at the beach with surfing, instead make it be in the mountains with skiing. You may not have to think about changing the ending, because so much will have changed already that it will change itself.

• Can you combine two personal narratives that interest you? Perhaps you can take something that happened to your father when he was young and update it so it could happen to a teenager today, and make the second part of the story be something that happened to you.

Don't forget, though, that since this is fiction, you need to change the names to protect the innocent. In my first novel, *A Space Apart*, I used a real-life story about an older woman, old enough to be my grandmother. In fact, I thought she was so old she must be dead by now, and I used not only some facts from her life, but her real name. It turned out that she was alive and when my novel was published, she read it and had her feelings hurt. I wish now that I had played a little more What If with that part of the novel. For my next novel, I was very careful not to use any real names.

WRITING MONOLOGUE

One last way to move your story along (and perhaps to find out more of what it is really about) is to explore what the characters are thinking. Whenever a story is told by an "I," it is called "first person," but sometimes, even if the story is told with "he" and "she," we still go into character's minds and find out what they are thinking.

I have already mentioned that often there is a conflict inside a single character. Sometimes characters think over what has happened to them, what is happening to them. They aren't speaking aloud to another person; instead, the reader is in the character's head, overhearing thoughts. They may be telling stories from their lives or describing the thoughts and conflicts happening to them at this very instant. This is called "interior monologue." If the interior monologue comes out as one thing associated with another, maybe sounding irrational or ungrammatical, we usually call it "stream of consciousness." Here is what is going on in the mind of a soldier as a bomb lands next to him:

"Who will it hit—Mikhaylov or me? Or both of us? And if me, whereabouts? If it's the head then I'm done for; but if it's the leg, they'll cut it off, and I'll certainly ask for chloroform and I may survive. But maybe only Mikhaylov will be hit, then I'll be able to tell how we were walking side by side, and he was killed and I was splashed with blood. No, it's nearer me...it'll be me." Then he remembered the twelve roubles he owed Mikhaylov, remembered also a debt in Petersburg which should have been paid long ago; a gypsy song he had sung the night before came into his head; the woman he loved appeared in his imagination wearing a bonnet with lilac ribbons.... "But perhaps it won't explode," he thought, and with a desperate resolve tried to open his eyes. But at that moment a red fire pierced his eyes through his still closed eyelids and something struck him in the middle of the chest with a terrible crash; he started to run, stumbled over a sword under his feet and fell on his side.[20]

Seven Steps to a Finished Story: Step Five

Add to your story a part where you go inside the head of one of your characters. This passage might be a first-person narrative or something more like the interior monologue example above.

Example

When I was back in Tennessee, everyone used to say, "Girl, you so pretty. You ought to be a TV actress or model." Well, yes, I am still that pretty girl, but I didn't turn out to be a television actress or model. I do more than that. I'm out here strictly to please the male gender. I stand on corners. Mainly 42nd and 6th. I parade up and down until one of those men see how pretty I am. They say, "Hey, pretty, why don't you jump in," and I usually do. Why do you do what you do, you may ask. Well, I ran away from Tennessee when I was thirteen. Only because I couldn't get along with those people down there. They were too country down there. I said, "Pretty (that's what I call myself), you have to get out of this hick town." So it was either New York or California. New York it was, and New York it is.

I've been on these streets for two years now, and I don't like it. Not at all! But what is one to do. The name of the game is survival. And I plan to survive! When I arrived at the Port Authority two years ago, I was scared out of my wits. That was the first time in my life that I was actually frightened. You would be too if you were there. A lot of homeless people were lying around, and a lot of kids were buzzing around. It was 4:37 A.M. I couldn't believe all the children that were out at that time of night. In Tennessee, children who were sixteen and younger had a curfew of 9:00 P.M. So you know I was stunned when I saw all of those children out that late. . . .

—Caprice Clark, 9th grade

• Try another passage of the thoughts of your character (or Caprice's) later in the story. It might be good to do after this character has been in a conflict. What does the character think about what has happened?

OTHER THINGS TO DO

• Write a conflict dialogue from real life that you have overheard in the last couple of days, even if it's about something totally boring, like your two cousins fighting over what program to watch on television. The conflict dialogue could be something you overheard on the street or at the mall or in the school lunchroom or something from your family.

• Take this real-life conflict and continue it fictionally. What might happen? Feel free to change it any way you like.

• Write a fiction dialogue with a friend. Each of you picks a character and you discuss what the characters' personalities are like. Then you write what your character says, and your partner answers, in writing.

• Do the same thing, but tape record it. *Then* copy it down in writing. How is it different from the one above?

• Write a conversation between two very different people. Perhaps one is rich and one is poor. Perhaps one talks a lot and one says little:

> The fat man . . . wore a black cutaway coat, black vest, black satin ascot tie holding a pinkish pearl, striped grey worsted trousers, and patent-leather shoes.
> His voice was a throaty purr. "Ah, Mr. Spade," he said with enthusiasm and held out a hand like a fat pink star. . . . The fat man raised

his glass and held it against a window's light. He nodded approvingly at the bubbles running up in it. He said: "Well, sir, here's to plain speaking and clear understanding."

They drank and lowered their glasses.

The fat man looked shrewdly at Spade and asked: "You're a close-mouthed man?"

Spade shook his head. "I like to talk."

"Better and better!" the fat man exclaimed. "I distrust a close-mouthed man. He generally picks the wrong time to talk and says the wrong things. Talking's something you can't do judiciously unless you keep in practice." He beamed over his glass. "We'll get along, sir, that we will." He set his glass on the table and held the box of Coronas del Ritz out to Spade. "A cigar, sir."

Spade took a cigar, trimmed the end of it, and lighted it. Meanwhile, the fat man pulled another green plush chair around to face Spade's within convenient distance and placed a smoking-stand within reach of both chairs. Then he took his glass from the table, took a cigar from the box, and lowered himself into his chair. His bulbs stopped jouncing and settled into flabby rest. He sighed comfortably and said, "Now, sir, we'll talk if you like. And I'll tell you right out that I'm a man who likes talking to a man that likes to talk."

"Swell. Will we talk about the black bird?"

The fat man laughed and his bulbs rode up and down on his laughter: "Will we?" he asked, and, "We will," he replied. His pink face was shiny with delight. "You're the man for me, sir, a man cut along my own lines. No beating around the bush, but right to the point. 'Will we talk about the black bird?' We will. I like that, sir. I like that way of doing business. Let us talk about the black bird by all means, but first, sir, answer me a question, please, though maybe an unnecessary one, so we'll understand each other from the beginning...."[21]

Example

Setting: A busy subway during rush hour.

Junkie of a very low class bumps into a very solemn man of a very rich family on his way home. He is rather grouchy in a proper way. The junkie has his Walkman radio on and a ripped leather jacket and dirty Adidas sneakers. He thinks he's cool and *bad!*

"Excuse me, but I think you had better watch where you are going, young man, this is a perfectly new suit and I do not intend to have *your* slimy hands all over it!" The solemn man said this roughly in a slight English accent.

"Yo man I did not touch you, anyways will you shut up, this is my favorite song, you know man? I really dig it." The junkie started to walk away, but stopped as if he remembered something. "Hey man, I just noticed my name is Joe and it is not 'Young Man.'" He said this sarcastically. "My hands are not dirty, and if you want to fight about it, I'm down."

"Why I never! I think I *will* call the police. I have never put up with such nonsense. Good day, Joe!"

"Eh, man, anytime, anytime." They both walk in different directions and forget all about it.

—Maya Newton, 5th grade

• Turn one of the dialogues you have written into a play, using proper dialogue form with stage instructions, etc.

Example

SETTING: A BUSY SUBWAY DURING RUSH HOUR

CAST: JUNKIE . . . . OF VERY LOW CLASS
        SOLEMN MAN . . . . RICH, WEARING NEW SUIT

ACT I: JUNKIE HAS ON HIS WALKMAN RADIO.
        HE BUMPS INTO THE SOLEMN MAN.

SOLEMN MAN

Excuse me, but I think you had better watch where you are going, young man, this is a perfectly new suit and I do not intend to have *your* slimy hands all over it!

JUNKIE

Yo man I did not touch you!

• Try it as a radio drama, remembering that nothing can be seen and everything has to be heard. Include instructions for sound effects.

• If you or one of your friends is good at drawing, try one as a comic strip or book.

• Have someone act out the dialogue you wrote that interests you most. After you've seen it acted, add things that the actors put in, such as ad-libbed jokes or gestures. This may also give you a new idea for how to end it. Anywhere an idea comes from is fine.

• Do a stream of consciousness piece for your character while he or she is walking to school, taking a shower, riding the bus, falling asleep.

• Make a class self-portrait using interior monologues of class members. Can people guess who is who?

LOOKING AGAIN: ORGANIZING

• Imagine if someone asked you to tell your story in twenty-five words or fewer. Actually, I hate it when someone does this to me, but it's one way of seeing if your story makes any kind of sense. Sometimes you can actually figure out the ending this way, too.

- Here's a story for young kids that has something pretty obviously wrong with it:

> Our dog Crush was as large as a pony and as black as pavement. We always used to think she was lazy, but then one day my little brother was playing in the middle of the street. No one saw him but Crush. Suddenly, a big delivery truck came at him like a freight train! Crush leaped to her feet and sprang out into the street. She grabbed my little brother by the shirt and pulled him to safety! By the way, Crush had one white paw.

The "by the way" means that the writer had another idea at the last minute. Everyone thinks up more ideas and better ideas as they write, but beginning writers often stick in their new ideas at the end, or somewhere else. That's fine when you are writing in a journal or making a first draft: PUT YOUR IDEAS DOWN ANYWHERE, ANYTIME. Then, when it comes time to look again and revise, be ready to move things around.

- Read over your "Seven Steps" story so far. You should have a beginning with some descriptions and a couple of passages of dialogue and monologue from later in the story. It may seem jerky, because you've been writing fragments, one at a time. Can you make an outline of it so far? For example:

1. A room in a shack in the woods.
2. Olon the Wolf Boy comes in and looks around, eats some dried meat.
3. The old man who lives in the shack comes home.
4. The old man yells and threatens.

5. Olon's stream of consciousness: how things look to him.
6. Information about the old man.
7. Information about Olon.
8. A few days later.

As you make the outline, you may say to yourself that it would be better if, say, the information about the old man were to come as he is walking home instead of in the middle of his yelling at the Wolf Boy. Try using scissors and tape (the way I suggested in the Looking Again section of chapter 6) to put parts of your story where they would work better. Cut out paragraphs and lay them on new sheets of paper with lots of space for adding ideas.

If you have a computer with word processing—especially what they call a "cut and paste" function—this is even easier. For example, you can easily move a whole paragraph of background narration from the end of the story to the beginning. I have moved paragraphs a lot as I get new ideas for this book.

In this chapter, I've suggested different ways to figure out what happens next in your story. You may have actually found out what your story is *about*. Sometimes when we start writing, we already have an idea or a subject, and sometimes the idea might work better written as nonfiction, as in the next chapter.

If you are near the end of your story, or very eager to get to the end of it, you might skip chapter 8 for now and go on to chapter 9, which is about finishing your story.

WHAT'S YOUR OPINION?

Nonfiction

TWO WAYS OF THINKING ABOUT CONFLICT

When you write fiction, you almost always tell the story of a person with a conflict. The conflict might be between two people, between a person and nature, or even within a person, but there is almost always a person with a problem. And when you set out to imagine a particular boy with a particular problem, you may be mainly interested in the boy, but you probably also have some opinions in the back of your mind about how he should act.

For example, imagine you write a story and your main character is the star pitcher on a high school baseball team. He has to decide whether or not he will use cocaine before he pitches. The boy's friends convince him the drug will make him pitch better. He tries it, he feels terrific, and he wins the game with his ace pitching. The guy thinks he is on top of the world, but he has one friend, maybe his girl friend, who quietly tells him that she won't be his friend anymore if he goes on like this. Maybe he never listens to her, or maybe he does. You might not even say that you think high school students should stay away from drugs, but the way you write about the conflict will show indirectly what your opinion is.

If you had written about this same material in an essay, you would have been very direct about what you thought. At some point you would have said explicitly that you don't believe drugs and high school athletics mix. You might have begun by telling briefly the very same story of the star baseball pitcher. Perhaps he started using cocaine to sharpen his game, and then he started throwing games in order to make money to buy the drug, and finally even lost his ability to play well. This narration would serve to support your opinion. You might also include in your essay a description of the effect of cocaine—information you may have researched. But your information, your descriptions, and your narration are all aimed at proving that cocaine is dangerous.

An "opinion essay" doesn't have to be about a big topic like drugs. Look at the letters-to-the-editor column of your local paper. You will see complaints about everything from dogs that dirty the park to the way teens wear their hair. Everyone has opinions. Often these essays are what we call pet peeves: you may want to tell the world what you think about parents who take away privileges unfairly or teachers who give a lot of homework in May and June. One of *my* favorite complaints is about people who talk to you while they wear sunglasses and you can't tell what their eyes are doing.

Opinion essays can express complaints, but they can also make a suggestion about how to do something or to persuade people to do something. You might, for example, write a speech for someone running for office. The point of your composition would be Why You Should Vote for Josephine Blowsephine. Another type of opinion essay is the review, in which you describe anything from a restaurant to a pair of sneakers to a movie or book and say why or in what ways it is good and bad. Another type of opinion essay is the "thinking" essay. In this type, you don't so much try to convince someone as you try to figure out what you think. Writing is a way of figuring out what your opinion is.

COMPLAINING

Everyone has something to complain about. We write notes to friends in other towns complaining about our families and schools.

We write formal letters to companies about faulty products and bad services. Some college students I know planned a letter-to-the-editor of their college newspaper to say they didn't think it was fair for members of the football team to get to choose their classes before the regular students.

• In your idea journal, make a list of things that irritate you. Choose one from your list and do a freewrite for about ten or fifteen minutes. Try to think of several times when this thing bothered you, and exaggerate how irritating it can be. Don't try to organize it. Using sentences or phrases, just write everything you can think of on the subject.

• *On a different day* (or at least several hours later) go back over your freewrite and turn it into an essay. Here's how:

FIRST look for a good example in the freewrite as a lead to catch the reader's attention:

> Have you ever put your hand under a table in a restaurant and felt something dry and curled up there and had a sinking feeling in the pit of your stomach?

NEXT, state clearly what you are complaining about:

> I have never been able to bear people who pick their noses in public places. When they leave their pickings behind them, they are really behaving antisocially.

THEN write a new paragraph with several more examples in the form of small stories—anecdotes or narratives—that prove your point.

FINALLY write an ending paragraph that summarizes your reasons and ENDS with a strong concluding sentence:

In conclusion, this is a habit that may be okay for babies, but anyone over the age of two should know better. Carry a Kleenex in your pocket. Use your tee shirt. Use anything but the tables and chairs and curtains and doors that *I* use. If some people don't stop this disgusting habit, I am afraid that other people like me will develop an equally disgusting habit: throwing up.

- Make a list of several products or services that have displeased you recently. Did the Red Rose tea box fail to have the miniature statue of a jungle beast in it? When you opened the pack of underwear, was it one pair short? Choose a complaint and write a polite letter to the Customer Service department of the company. If there is nothing on the product that has an address, ask the reference librarian for a book called *Standard and Poor's Register*, which has the addresses of most major companies. Also send a copy of your letter to the Chamber of Commerce or Better Business Bureau of the city where the company is located.

WRITING A REVIEW

If you take a look in the arts and leisure or entertainment section of your newspaper, you will find reviews of books, movies, TV shows, plays, new albums and videos, live performances of rock and classical groups. In many colleges and some secondary schools, even professors and teachers get reviewed by their students. Teachers, of course, give their students short reviews called grades.

- Choose something to review. Here's a hint: the most boring reviews to read are the ones that have nothing but gushing praise in them, so you might want to choose a restaurant or movie that you like some things about but not everything. *Visit* the restaurant (or see the movie, or read the book) and while it is fresh in your mind, *take notes*. Do a directed freewrite on it for about ten minutes. When reviewing a book, I always put my notes directly into my journal, writing my first impressions, even if they include words I might not want to publish in the final version.

Begin the review with *essential information*. Reviews always start with certain basic facts. That is, if it is a movie, give the title, rating, director, and main actors; if it's a book, give its price and publisher as well as title and author. For a restaurant, you would begin with its name and location, its type (fast food, Chinese health food, pizza family restaurant?) and its price range.

Once you have the basic facts, you are ready to *describe* it. If it's a book or movie, tell something about the plot (but try not to give away the ending). If it's a restaurant, tell something about the decorations—is it fancy with white tablecloths? Does it have soft music playing all the time? Use all your senses, including, of course, the sense of taste. What tastes good and bad in Fribble's? Are the hot fudge sundaes a sublime experience, but the malted milk shakes too thin? In the description paragraph, you can begin to give your opinion: if you talk about mostly delicious things, then the reader has a pretty good idea that you are going to give an overall favorable review. If, along with describing your favorite ice creams, you mention that the owner is always frowning at anyone in her restaurant under the age of thirty, then a reader is learning that while it might be a great place for ice cream, you may not want to plan on hanging out there for a few hours with your fifteen best friends.

After the description is finished, *summarize* your opinion of the restaurant:

In conclusion, arrive at Fribble's with an empty stomach, a fat wallet, and your best behavior. This fancy ice cream restaurant has the best sundaes in town by far, but the price tag is not cheap, and the owner does not welcome rowdiness.

• Try a review of something else. If you reviewed a restaurant, try a movie now.

Example

I'm going to review *Slaughter High*. This movie was very exciting, but don't be fooled by its cover, because they make it look scary and disgusting, but it isn't. It is about a school that this one gang runs and tells people what to do. But then a new kid comes and teaches them a lesson. But then the other kids started to run. The new kid was not too happy about it. It's not too scary and not too funny. I give it a 5 and a half.
—Erin Ross, 7th grade

• Write a review of this book. Would you recommend it to other people your age? What parts would you recommend or not? Why?

Examples

I really enjoyed reading your chapter. It had a lot of feelings. Most workbooks are boring and don't show emotions. This one made me feel like you were a friend trying to get my feelings out.
—Susan Lawra, 9th grade

I think this book would be good for someone who doesn't already enjoy writing. I really enjoy writing and structured books are not enjoyable for me to write with.
—Erica Schreiber, 10th grade

I like the parts where you make up your own stories. There should be more stories to read so someone can get ideas for the assignment.
—Andrea Ferreira, 7th grade

I love to write stories, but I like to make up my own topic. This chapter changed my mind. You have a wonderful way of mixing school and fun. I liked the way you gave an example for each type of writing and the way the assignments were mixed in the chapter instead of waiting until the end because if they are at the end, you have to go back in the chapter to see what the author is talking about.
—Jeff Scott, 9th grade

WRITING OPINIONS TO FIND OUT WHAT YOU THINK

I consider writing to be one of the best ways of figuring out your opinions. I'm not sure why this is true—our minds go all the time, thinking away, and when we talk with friends, we share views and maybe even change what we think about something as we talk. But there is nothing like writing down, freewrite or journal style, all your ideas on a subject, and then organizing them, to make yourself come to a conclusion.

There are many important public topics in the news that you may want to work through for yourself: capital punishment, gun control, teen suicide, the drinking age. There are other important topics to think about, too, because they may affect you very personally at any moment if they haven't already: sex and birth control, using drugs, wearing helmets when you ride a bicycle or ATV. *You may not know beforehand exactly where you stand on any of these issues.*

• Write an essay that gives your opinion on some subject you already know or have thought about.

Example

I am a skateboarder. Skateboarding takes up most of my time. I go almost every day. Most kids who skateboard like to learn new tricks. Learning a new trick gives a good feeling, a feeling of accomplishment. Especially when the trick is hard. If you really want to learn a lot of new tricks, you have to push yourself a little. As you get better, the tricks get harder, and you want to learn more tricks. Some tricks are way too hard for some kids, but these kids still try the hardest of tricks. All skateboarders try things and get lucky or fail.

When I go skateboarding, I try to learn as much as I can, but I don't try tricks I know I can't do. It is also not a good idea to skateboard when you're tired or not able to concentrate, because you could get hurt. The whole point to this story is, don't try things you know you can't do. Everyone can relate to that, no matter who you are or what you do. Always take into consideration your abilities. *Especially* if you're a skateboarder.

—Bryan Smith, 9th grade

* Pretend you write a column called "A Teen Talks to Teens." Someone writes a letter to you saying:

I am thirteen years old. I fell in love last summer with John (not his real name). He is twenty-one years old. My parents told me he was too old for me and this is just "puppy love." But I still love him. We have begun to do all the things that married people do, and I love him more each day. He wants me to leave home and move into an apartment with him. I am no longer interested in school. I feel I am a woman. What should I do?

Now you have to respond to this letter writer. Whatever you do, don't answer quickly, without giving it some thought. Don't say what you think your father would say, or your priest or preacher or rabbi. Freewrite for fifteen minutes about this girl's situation. Then start to pull out of your freewrite what you think are your best thoughts. Remember that there may not be just one answer. Remember that you yourself may have mixed feelings. Write an answer to the girl.

• Think of someone you know, your age, with personal dilemmas or problems with families or friends. Pretend to be this person and write a letter to the Teen Advisor, then write the answer, using the freewrite-first technique of finding out what you think.

Example

Dear Erica,
   I have a problem that is getting way out of control. I just moved to a new school last year. I really wanted everyone to like me. I was so afraid people wouldn't like me, so I made up stories and lies about myself. The lies are getting more and more complex. To make it even worse there is one person who knows the truth. She has always kept quiet, but now she's threatening to tell everything! What should I do?
                                          Signed,
                                          Liar

Dear Liar,

I know now you are scared that if everyone finds out the truth they will all hate you. Lies only complicate things. If you don't tell the truth, it will be harder and harder to tell the truth in the future, and these lies could turn into something much bigger. I think your only choice is to tell everyone the truth and hope for the best. Your friendships are all based on lies. The longer y,u wait, the harder it will be to start anew. Some people will have probably been in a similar position and will understand. Good luck. Always remember that honesty is always the best option.

Sincerely,
Erica

—Erica Schreiber, 10th grade

• Have the president of the United States write a letter about some national or international problem to the Teen Advisor. Using freewriting, try to give him some help on arms control or how to cut the budget or whatever he asks you.

OTHER THINGS TO DO

• With a friend, take turns being the person with the problem and the advisor. Write to one another.

• See if you can get friends and family to send letters to your advice column. If you have access to a typewriter or word processor, publish your advice column. You can be serious or funny or both.

• Write a real letter-to-the-editor about some topic that you feel strongly about.

LOOKING AGAIN: ORGANIZING A FIVE-PARAGRAPH ESSAY

Often as you go through school, you will be asked to write your opinion in a particular form known as the Five-Paragraph Essay (we'll call it "the 5-PE" for short). If you can learn how to write this type of opinion essay easily, you will possess an ever-handy tool (a little like a Swiss Army knife) for all sorts of school situations, particularly testing. People who make standardized tests love the 5-PE because it is an easy way to see if the student followed directions. It will also come in handy for the day you decide you have to write to the editor of your local paper to tell exactly what you think of the mayor or the school system or the guy who wrote last week to criticize the football team.

• The first thing you need for a 5-PE is an opinion on something. Choose an opinion you've already written about, or think up a new one. It doesn't have to be the most profound opinion in the world. You might even want to do, for this practice essay, "As pets, guppies are superior to all others." Write a short paragraph that begins with an anecdote or some description (perhaps of the sweet guppies swimming around in their little fish bowl). "I will always remember the day I bought my first guppy." Whatever else it says, the paragraph has to say somewhere, "Guppies make the best pets." This is called your "thesis sentence." It is your main idea or opinion. The paragraph needs one more thing. It also needs to say what the rest of the essay is going to say. You might end the paragraph with something like, "Guppies make the best pets because of their cleanliness, inexpensiveness, and friendliness." This gives you a really good hint of what paragraphs two, three, and four are supposed to be about. By the time you've finished the first paragraph of the 5PE, your hardest work is over.

• Next write Paragraph Two, which tells about (you guessed it) how *clean* guppies are. You need an example of how their bowl never gets dirty. You could quote from a book about guppies, and you could also mention by comparison how disgusting a cat's used litter box is.

• Paragraph Three is about (how did you guess?) how *cheap* guppies are. You can tell the price at a local store and maybe also, for contrast, the price of a full-bred golden retriever puppy. Write Paragraph Three.

• Now hit the reader with your best reason: "Guppies are the friendliest of all pets! They never scratch, growl, or have to go to the vet." You will, of course, have some cute story to tell here about how your favorite guppy Gertrude always comes right to the top of the water whenever you sprinkle fish food there. Write Paragraph Four.

• The final paragraph, Paragraph Five, says what you've already said, but in a different way: "In conclusion, there is nothing like a guppy. Dogs cost a lot of money, cats have smelly litter boxes, rabbits don't miss you if you go on vacation. But guppies are clean, inexpensive, and loving. Guppies make the best pets of all." Write Paragraph Five.

That's it: the 5-PE. First, it tells what it is going to say; it says it; it summarizes what it said. It's neat, it's clear, and they love to put it on big tests.

If you can express your opinions thoughtfully and precisely, you'll go far in the world of school. The best way to finish a piece of fiction or a personal essay, however, is not always so obvious.

CHAPTER 9

FINISHING

Fiction

COMPLETING A STORY

Finishing a story is hard. Oh, if you get bored, you can always have your characters suddenly fall off a cliff or get married. If it's a fantasy, you can say, "And then I woke up. It was all a dream." But those aren't really *completions*, to my way of thinking. They are just signs that the writer wanted to go play softball or make popcorn.

How do we make—or find—the real ending?

Let me say here that I don't believe everything has to be finished. If you really aren't interested in a story, lay it aside. Don't throw it away, because you may decide to use it later. Besides, some things were meant to be fragments, journal entries, little anecdotes or vignettes.

On the other hand, there is a lot to be said for the feeling of finishing something, even if it isn't perfect. I like to get a rough draft done, so I can get a look at the whole thing. I finished the first draft of my science fiction novel, but the last chapter is awful. I mean really awful. Still, I have an idea now of what's going to happen in the end, and I can take a rest with a feeling of accomplishment.

I think, when you come down to it, the best way to finish a story is to let your imagination wander around, then write until you run out of steam, take a break, and go back to it. The break can be pretty long sometimes. I had the idea for my science fiction novel when I was just starting high school, but I didn't feel like finishing it then. I used to write little bits of description or dialogue for it when the mood hit me, but I didn't actually finish a draft until twenty-five years later. I'm not recommending you wait so long, but sometimes it takes patience to figure out what you really want to say in fiction.

To help you complete your story draft, I don't have a formula or plan to follow like the 5-PE. Exercises and assignments are great for getting started and getting ideas, but the best endings come out of the writing itself. In any case, here are some more general ways to finish a story.

FINISHING A STORY
BY THE "KITCHEN TIMER" METHOD

Seven Steps to a Finished Story: Step Six.

I talked in chapter 7 about making a blank movie screen in your mind to see what happens next. This next technique is even simpler. Once a day, set an alarm clock or kitchen timer for anything from ten minutes to an hour (an hour is too much for most people), and during that time add on to your story. Be reasonable: if every day is too often for you, write twice a week, or every Saturday morning—just be sure and set yourself a time you think you can actually sit through. Using the timer is important because it will help you sit for the full amount of time. If you like to write, you probably have times when you *have* to write, when inspiration practically knocks you across the room. The trick is how to keep yourself going, once the inspiration has died down.

Here are a couple of sample patterns:

A. Every morning for a week in the summer, at 9 A.M., with your English muffin and orange juice beside you, write for fifteen minutes.

B. Monday, Wednesday, and Friday write for twenty minutes when you get home from school (or before you go to bed).

C. Every Saturday morning, write for one hour while the cartoons are on (for background noise).

Always use the same place for writing, a place you like, whether it is the kitchen table or the top bunk in your little brother's room or a special bench in the park near the hot dog stand. Some sessions you will probably write well, sometimes it may be crummy stuff. If you really get going, write as long as you feel like it, but don't ever sit for less than the time you've allotted. If you can't think of anything to write, *you still have to sit there.* Doodle or twirl your hair, but make yourself stay at the desk or table or in your bed or wherever you like to write until the timer goes off. Sometimes being bored will make your mind come up with something. This is very important, because one of the ways writers write is by getting themselves so bored by staring at the paper or computer screen that they finally start to work. I'm not kidding. I've done it.

After a couple of sessions, there is a really good chance you will come up with a solution to the problem, or an outcome to the conflict—something that will allow you to write The End, at least for now.

THE OUTLINE METHOD OF FINISHING

• Another way to finish is to use the outline-in-progress. This is not the outline in which you plan everything in advance. The idea here is to get a good start and *then* make a plan. Look back over what you've written so far and scribble down what's there (for an example, see the Looking Again section of chapter 7). Add a few words about what might come next. Remember that you can always change your mind later. This is something I almost always do with a long story or book, because there is too much to keep in my head at one time. I write a lot of pages (but I don't finish) and then I step back and look at what I've done and write an outline.

An outline can be long and complicated or very short, just hints. Here's part of a fairly detailed one. Notice that I don't really pay much attention to standard outline form, because what I'm doing is just making notes about what I've already written and ideas for things to add later:

Outline-in-Progress

Chapter I: General history, religion, the Battle for the Coast Land, etc. (5 pages)

Chapter II: Espere, her father and mother. Father arrives too early in spring, almost dead of exposure. They revive him. He needs someone to deliver a message, which her mother does not want her to do. Espere wants to. *ADD that her father promises there will be no killing.*

Chapter III: Espere crosses the desert. About to die from lack of food, she smells wet air. Meets Chorine, is shocked by slavery and cruelty. *Put in about drugs.*

As you see, I call it an "outline-in-progress," because I change it every few weeks. It is sort of a thumbnail sketch of what happens in each part, with new ideas to add. Whenever I make a change as I am writing, I put it into the outline. When I come up with an idea for something new, I put that in too.

In my novel, people's names change all the time. The main animal on the planet started out to be a sort of dragon that people rode, then I changed it to a thing like a flying dinosaur, and now it is something I call a "yaeger," a sort of a giant pterodon with wings and razor blades. I keep the old outlines with the date I wrote them, because it's fun for me to go back and see what I used to think, and sometimes I decide the old idea is better than the new one.

FINISH IT BY CONSULTING WITH FRIENDS ABOUT THE PLOT

• This is pretty much self-explanatory. Take the five, six, ten, or however many pages you've written and read them aloud to a group of friends, or give them to one friend. Get the friends to say what they think will happen. Then tell them what *you* think, and get their reactions and suggestions. I belong to a group that meets every two weeks except in the summer. We take turns reading and critiquing one another's work, and one of the things we do is make suggestions about what should happen. We don't always take one another's advice, but the fresh ideas always give us new ideas of our own.

OTHER THINGS TO DO

Here are some starter ideas that give you a ready-made plot so that you aren't left floundering for how to end it. Some people like to write a story that has a complete plot worked out from the very beginning. They might spend weeks never writing a word, but creating the story in their mind. Other people make detailed lists of when things happen in the story and write them on long pieces of paper that they tape all over their walls. Here are some ways to write stories with built-in endings.

• You might read in the newspaper about some crime that catches your attention. Maybe there was a ring of teenagers arrested for shoplifting. Your story could start with the arrests (in other words, the ending comes first) and then tell how these particular kids came to this sorry end.

• The personal problems of a friend of yours (the sort of thing we used in the "Teen Talks to Teens" imaginary advice column) and how the friend solved the problem might give you a story about what the situation was and how it got resolved.

• Write a story based on the real life story of a person. You know the general facts of how they lived and died; now change a few things to make it fiction.

• A dream could provide a plot for a story. I wrote a story called "The Siege of the Lake" directly from a dream I had. It came ready-made with a sort of weird ending that I liked.

• Write a story in which some minor character tells what happened from her or his point of view. If it is something from history, you already know the ending (a soldier riding in the boat with George Washington crossing the Delaware; a slave on a plantation in Georgia during the Civil War; a mate on the *U.S.S. Thresher* submarine just before it sank), so you can concentrate on what this made-up character experiences. Does General Washington treat you fairly? Do you escape and join the northern armies? Are you brave as your ship goes down?

Extract from the *U.S.S. Thresher's* First Mate's Diary

The alarm just went off, and the crew is running from station to station. We are rapidly sinking. We're 910 feet below the surface. I can hear groans from the hull as it strains from the pressure. I imagine that I can see the hull beginning to implode. The sub is pitching and we're taking on a list to port. The radio is out, and the technicians are frantically trying to repair it.

I can smell an electrical fire from aft. The chief engineer is shouting for more power. Some idiot is shutting down the reactor—something about the flood-water. I try to tell him to open the auxiliary valves, but he won't listen.

The bulkhead doors are swinging shut and I am trapped. The pressure on the hull is mounting. I know I will not survive. I try not

to panic, but it is no use. Suddenly I am pounding on the bulkhead door. It won't open. The water is coming in now. It is freezing. People are shouting. I. . . .
—David Parichy, 6th grade

• Try writing the real life story of a famous person in the first person: as if you were the person. You know all the facts, and what you have to make up is how the person feels about the things that happen.

• Write a fiction story that takes place in a real country you might have come from or visited, like Brazil. Use your own real life experiences, following along the actual things that happened, so you know how the trip begins, what the high points are, how it ends.

LOOKING AGAIN: ENDING

• Write three alternate last sentences for your story. Lay the sentences aside for a few hours or few days, then choose the best one.

• Reread your story and write a short opinion or review of it. What is best about it? What would you like to know more about? Does the ending seem true? After some time has passed, reread your review and see if you want to make any changes in the story based on it.

Seven Steps to a Finished Story: Step Seven

Do something to celebrate finishing the story. Type it up (or have a friend type it) and then make some xerox copies. Send it to friends and relatives and ask for reactions. Submit it to your school newspaper or literary magazine.

If you and a couple of friends finish stories about the same time, make a little book of your stories together, perhaps with illustrations.

Give a reading to a select invited audience of friends and family.

Tape the readings and offer them to be played wherever it might be appropriate: to young kids, to people in a nursing home, etc.

Be proud of what you've accomplished.

Keep writing.

Irita Mullins

A Story by Meredith Sue Willis When She Was Fifteen

I had ruined my shoes in the moist red clay before I was halfway up Bald Indian Mountain. Beyond Joe Strange's farm the trees closed in so that the August sun was hidden, and I was in a cool twilight. When I saw a little snake cross my path, I began to wish I had let Joe send his boy up the mountain with me.

I was going up to Zeke Mullins's farm that August afternoon to fulfill a promise I had made in the spring of the same year, before school was out. I was a bride of one month, and my husband Dick Pharow was in the city several hundred miles away. Dick is a lawyer, and he refused to let me go on teaching. ("The woman I marry," he said a thousand times, and then "My wife," another thousand, "is going to be Mrs. Dick Pharow, nobody else.") That was why I was going up the mountain to get Irita Mullins.

The first time I saw Irita was in my little one-room schoolroom that first and last year of my teaching. I was getting along wonderfully well with the neighborly hill-people and their children. Most of them managed to visit me with offerings of cake and pie and fresh vegetables at least once a week, because they were somewhat worried about a single woman living by herself. Their children were not perhaps the most brilliant of pupils, but they had a healthy interest in life and living things that I have never seen even in exceptional city children.

It was the third week of school. One morning Willie Willis wandered in an hour late with a baby groundhog he had caught in one of his traps. That was his excuse for tardiness. All of us were clustered around my desk, and Willie was giving me some facts on the habits of "whistle pigs." Suddenly the class grew tense and Willie stopped his talk. "It's Mullinses," a little girl whispered.

Indeed, the population of the schoolroom had been increased by at least eight of the dirtiest, most dull looking urchins I had ever seen. My eyes rested on them only briefly, for I saw Irita. I still cannot imagine how Zeke Mullins and his zombie-like wife ever produced Irita. There is a saying that Mullinses only marry Mullinses—who else would have them?—and the constant inbreeding had created a family of pale half-wits in the finest white trash tradition. But Irita was different. She must have been about fourteen at the time—the oldest living Mullins child—but she already towered well above my five feet five inches, and she was built like a goddess. Her hair was a long, violently black mass and she had extremely heavy but well-shaped eyebrows; they half hid her bright eyes.

She carried herself, there in the midst of those lice-infested, dirt-encrusted vermin, like a queen. She wore a gray feed sack rag, much too small for her, yet she could have been wearing ermine, so proud and dignified she was. I compared her in my mind to what a Valkyrie should look like. "We come to school," she said.

For a whole month the Mullins brood came to school. They sat at desks and slept or fidgeted. It was obvious that the only reason they were there at all was Irita. I couldn't teach them. Most of them could hardly speak English and at last Irita too realized that school was not for them. When she left them at home, I was able at last to sleep without worrying if I had contracted some horrible parasite the preceding day.

But Irita kept coming, and she brought one little brother, five-year-old Rastus. Rastus was, no doubt, quite as moronic as the rest of his family, but somehow I had to like Rastus. Perhaps he had had an extra measure of affection from Irita, because she had nursed him after he was burnt. When he was three or four, he had stood too near the stove and caught on fire. Zeke would not call a doctor, and eventually Rastus's burns had healed, but he was left horribly disfigured. The raw wounds around his neck and chest had been converted to a tough scar tissue that was not elastic enough for free movement, and as a result, his mouth never quite closed and his eyes and nose were stretched out of shape. When he smiled, the whole mass of twisted visage writhed, and I felt like crying or throwing up. But he was a sweet child.

Irita was the oldest child in the class, because all of the children above fourth grade went into town to the "big school." She didn't fit into the seats, and her clothes were outrageous, but she came. And she learned to read in less than six weeks. I kept telling myself that since she was older she would naturally learn faster, but when she finished the third grade reader before Christmas, I finally realized that Irita could only be a genius. She asked me to give her special lessons during lunch hour and recess and we studied and studied. She seemed to be positively starved for knowledge, but she rarely asked questions. Anything I said, she accepted as gospel truth. Kay, I told myself, you have been presented with the perfect student. A pure and unsullied intellect, with no knowledge of the world and no precedents. I prayed that I would teach this virgin mind well.

Only once did Irita break out of her self-contained coldness. That was the day Willie and the children laughed at Rastus. Irita and I were in the schoolroom reading from a simple novel when we heard the laughter and went to see what was so hilarious. Willie isn't a cruel little boy. He reminds me of Huckleberry Finn, with a lot of scientific curiosity thrown in. For lack of anything better to do, Willie had given Rastus a piece of a caramel candy "just to see how the poor young'un chawed." The little boy had to use both hands to close his gaping mouth, and then he couldn't open it. He struggled and groaned and gasped and choked, but the candy held fast. All of the children gathered round to see his interesting contortions. Great tears began to roll down Rastus's cheeks. When Irita saw Rastus, she turned white and pushed through the children roughly. She opened Rastus's mouth, extracted the caramel and flung it on the ground. "Who give him that candy?" she asked icily.

Willie swallowed hard and said, "Me."

Irita seized Willie's hair with one hand and with the other slapped him until blood trickled from the corner of his mouth. He didn't resist, because hill boys don't hit women.

"Irita," I cried. "Stop that!"

And after I had shooed the crowd into the building and sent Willie to the wash house, I asked her why she had attacked Willie so savagely.

"Ah'm a Mullins," she said, "And that boy hurt my brother."

All winter Irita and Rastus came down off the mountain through bitter cold and mud and snow. Often she could hardly hold a pencil because of her icy hands, but it took me three weeks to convince her that she would be foolish not to accept the gloves I offered her. Often she would stay at my little cottage after school for special lessons and I had an opportunity to feed her and Rastus and to instruct her in some of the basic ideas that are instilled in most of us from earliest childhood.

She could see no reason to take a bath, and, indeed, she had never had one. Hairbrushes and toothbrushes were a great novelty to her, though she accepted electricity as a sort of minor miracle that came naturally to those who could read and write. Science had little charm for her, because she was of an extremely matter-of-fact turn. She could not imagine atoms, and as for biology, she had seen quite enough of birth and death on the mountain.

But history and literature fascinated her. She received her most profound frustrations when statements were beyond her comprehension or when she did not know a word. I remember one blizzardy night that she and Rastus were forced to spend with me. That was the night I introduced the dictionary to her. I had bathed Rastus and put him in bed with me, giving Irita the living room couch. He smelled so good and so fresh and soft that I fell asleep dreaming that he was my own son and that Dick and I were finally married. I was so terribly snug that I was vaguely aware of the living room light being on for some time before I rose to investigate. When I finally did, I discovered Irita with the dictionary in the middle of the floor murmuring to herself.

"Irita," I said sleepily, "what *are* you doing?"

She started and looked panicky. "Oh, Miss Gates, Ah'm just readin' the dicshunerry. Ah figgered the best way to unnerstand all them books is to learn all of these here words. Did you know that a abb is some kind of yarn?"

"Oh, Irita, darling. No one can learn *all* of the words in it," I cried, partly amused and partly awed.

But she never quite believed me and I'd often find her in some obscure corner of the schoolroom or my cottage studiously memorizing the dictionary.

And I'll never forget the time I loaned her *Robinson Crusoe*. She didn't smile, but I could tell that she was about to burst with self-contained pleasure when I offered to let her take the book up the mountain one evening. She loved that book. There was something in one man's making a living from nothing that fascinated her.

Two days later she came to me and reported in a trembling voice that her father had got drunk and torn the book up. She faced me with closed eyes as if I were about to beat her. "Miss Gates," she whispered with bent shoulders, "he says papers is only fitten fo'—fo' toilet paper." The whole affair would have been comical if it hadn't been so tragic. But no one could laugh at Irita Mullins. She was the least funny person I had ever met.

I told her that I had meant to give the book to her anyhow, but she saw through my little lie. There was nothing else she could do, so she never took another book up the mountain.

That spring Irita came to school early and stayed late. Her search for knowledge became almost frantic. We talked, or rather I talked, of everything under the sun. I would say, "Irita, don't you have *any* questions?" and she would shake her head and reply, "I ain't got time. I got to hear everything so's Ah can have something to think on—later." That was a portentous statement though I didn't realize it at the time.

Then it was June and the school year was over. On the last day, after commencement exercises, when all of the proud parents had come up and discussed their children with me, only Irita, wearing an old white dress of mine that made her look older and prettier, and Rastus remained. Irita's hair was pulled out of her eyes with a pink ribbon and the hair had been brushed to a glowing brilliance. Rastus was clean and smiling his angelic caricature of a smile. "Well, Irita," I said, "I wish I were going to be here this summer. We could study right on, but I must go visit my mother and father." And Dick, I added mentally, but of course I didn't say so to Irita. I hadn't seen Dick for months, but he would keep writing and proposing to me. I will see him this summer, I thought, and tell him for the last time that I will not marry him, my teaching is more important.

Irita stared at Bald Indian Mountain and stroked Rastus's head. "Ah guess Ah won't be comin' back," she said quietly.

"Irita!" I gasped. "Why ever not?"

She shook her head. "Pa, he don't like books. An' Ma's right sickly. Someone's got to look after the young'uns."

"Don't you want to come?"

"Yes, ma'am. Ah do."

"Well, then, before school starts, I'll come up and see your father myself. I'll just talk to him myself and we'll see if he won't let you come to school. There are laws, you know."

Irita laughed. It was odd, thinking back, but I had never heard her laugh before, and this wasn't a pleasant laugh. "Pa," she said. "Pa ain't going to talk to nobody, Miss Gates. If Pa's sober, he run from you an' if he's drunk, he chase you."

"Well, just the same, I'll be up," I said bravely, "And I'll write to you and you must write to me, to keep in practice. Here is the address. Now you must promise to keep yourself and Rastus clean and to boil the water you drink and . . . ."

She almost smiled, and promised. Then she and Rastus started up the mountain. I'll never forget the way she walked. She stood very tall, and after a little way, she stopped to pick Rastus up and little Rastus looked over her shoulder and waved. Irita didn't look back.

*** *** ***

Of course once I did get home, and saw Dick, I decided that I wanted to be his wife more than I wanted to teach and we were married the first of July. I wrote to the Board of Education and resigned my post in the little one-room schoolhouse at the foot of Bald Indian Mountain, but Irita Mullins was constantly on my mind.

"Dick," I said carefully one evening, "you know since we're going to the city this fall and I'll be quite alone in the apartment, don't you think I might get a little lonely?"

"You'll have lots to do, honey. Parties, decorating, all that rot."

"I'm going to miss teaching."

"No, you won't. Besides, we'll be having some little pupils for you real soon anyway."

"Just the same I'd rather like to have someone to stay with me. In the big city and all."

"You've got me, baby."

"I know the nicest little girl," I said. "She could help with the housework and wouldn't cost anything at all hardly."

"Hmm...?" He was reading the *Wall Street Journal.*

"Then you mean I can, darling?"

"Can what?"

"Why, bring Irita to the city with us, of course."

"Who in the heck is Irita?"

But in the end we decided that she would come as a sort of combination maid-companion. Dick grumbled, but I wrote to Irita. This, I was sure, was her opportunity to get away from that mountain.

She wrote back on a smudged, but extremely neat slip of paper, Dear Miss Gates (though I'd told her about Dick), I am waiting for you. Rastus is fine. Your student, Irita Mullins.

And as I said before, that was why I was going up the mountain to get Irita Mullins. I finally found my way out of the forest and before me lay Zeke Mullins's farm. The cabin had the finest location of any home on the mountain; with pine forest behind it and the beautiful panorama of mountains before it. But the homestead itself was nothing more than a monstrous trash deposit. The yard was bare of grass and littered with bones, dogs, broken bottles, rags, chickens, and various organic wastes—some of which were suspiciously human. The wind changed and I received a whiff of the place. I had a distinct impulse to turn around and leave, but then I saw Irita.

She was standing as far from the house as was possible without stepping over the cliff that plunged several hundred feet to the river that ran past my schoolhouse. I was impressed as always by her splendid figure and her head was thrown back. I admired her for some minutes before I realized that she was about to jump from the cliff. I can't say how I knew, perhaps it was because I had been forced to interpret her ideas and emotions by the attitude of her body and the expression in her eyes, but somehow I sensed that she was seriously contemplating hurling herself into the air and falling to her death. Death! That did not seem to me to be a strange state for Irita at all; the Valkyries of whom she had reminded me so often were bearers of death.

There she stood and I not thirty yards from her, but I was mute and unable to tear myself away from the beauty of the picture before me. I don't know whether I would have cried out or if she would have changed her mind, because at that instant, a little figure stole up behind her unnoticed by me and tugged gently on her dress tail. It was Rastus.

She turned and looked at him as if he were a stranger, but the spell was broken, and I felt that the crisis was past. She lifted Rastus and kissed him with more gentleness than I had ever seen in her before.

Then I walked out of the trees and called, "Irita! Oh, Irita."

"Miss Gates!" she exclaimed with a sort of panic in her voice.

"Why, yes," I fumbled for words. What do you say to someone who nearly committed suicide? "I've come to get you—I mean—are you ready?"

She slowly looked at herself. She was wearing the white dress. It was soiled and torn under one arm and her hair had fallen awry from the pink ribbon. "Ah ain't goin'," she said gently.

My mouth fell open and I sputtered.

She faced me suddenly and told her story in one long burst of words. "Miss Gates, this mornin' Ah was ready to go. My clothes is ready and Ah told Rastus good-by and Ah was thinkin' how wonderful it would be in the city with you and we could see all those things you read to me about for real an' Ah even thought you might let me change my name to yours an', oh, Ah was happy. But this afternoon my Ma up an' died an' Ah knew Ah wasn't ever meant to go off the mountain." There were actually tears in her eyes. "Ah knew that them young'uns weren't never goin' to feed theirselves an' my Pa would most probly drink so much he'd die an' just before you came Ah was nigh onto jumpin' off that rock. But that wouldn't of helped, cause them kids would of starved same as if Ah'd left 'em. Ah cain't leave, Miss Gates. They need me."

As evidence of this Rastus hugged her leg and smiled at me.

"Irita," I said, "you can't do this. You have a great mind, and you can't bury it in—in THIS!"

Then Zeke Mullins himself came out of the cabin. "Hey, Irity," he whined. "Ah'm mahty hongry."

Irita didn't look at him. "You got to bury Ma afore Ah fix you somethin' to eat, Pa."

He was a little man, dirty and dissipated, if a person of such low intelligence can ever be said to lower himself more. "Aw, Irity," he began, but caught sight of me and clumped off into the woods with frequent backward glances.

"You see?" Irita cried, "You see? Ah even got to bury her. She wasn't no account; all she an' Pa ever did was lie around, but she was the only one that could make him do anything, an' now he go off to that still of his and drink till he die. Ah hope he does," she added savagely, "Ah hope he does."

I didn't know what to say. I was out of my element. This whole mad family—most of all Irita—and this depressing place seemed about to suffocate me in its filth and unreasonableness. "Irita—" I murmured faintly, "won't you change your mind?"

Her dark eyes began to smoulder, and she shook Rastus off roughly. There was no vestige of the tears that had lain in her eyes. She straightened her back and pulled her lips over her teeth in a sort of grin. "Ah'm staying, Miss Gates," she said. "Ah ain't never leavin' again."

For a moment I hesitated. What could I say? What could I do? She was so dignified and proud that I felt small and insignificant in the face of her sacrifice.

I left, pausing only once to see her for the last time. The sun was lowering in the west and she was in silhouette against the gold and orange. I shall never forget her splendidness, there alone on the mountain, a cut diamond in the midst of the filth.

Endnotes

[1] Meredith Sue Willis, "My Boy Elroy" in *PEN Short Story Collection* (New York: Ballantine Books, 1985)

[2] Montaigne, "Of Presumption" in *The Complete Works of Montaigne*, translated by Donald M. Frame (Stanford, CA: Stanford University Press, 1943)

[3] Anaïs Nin, *Linotte: The Early Diaries of Anaïs Nin* (New York: Harcourt Brace Jovanovich, 1978)

[4] Eldridge Cleaver, "A Day in Folsom Prison" in *Soul on Ice* (New York:Dell, 1968)

[5] Michael Ryan, "She Tells Tales for a Living," *Parade Magazine*, July 24, 1988

[6] Meredith Sue Willis, "Luis, a True Story" in *Journal of a Living Experiment*, edited by Philip Lopate (New York: Teachers & Writers Collaborative, 1979)

[7] Gertrude Stein, from "Portrait of Picasso" in *Selected Writings of Gertrude Stein*, edited by Carl Van Vechten (New York: Vintage Books, 1975)

[8] Meredith Sue Willis, *Higher Ground* (New York: Scribner's, 1981)

[9] Paulette Childress White, "Alice" in *Sturdy Black Bridges: Visions of Black Women in Literature*, edited by Roseann P. Bell, Bettye J. Parker, and Beverly Guy-Shaftall (Garden City, NY: Doubleday & Co., 1979)

[10] Tobias Smollet, *The Expedition of Humphry Clinker* (Baltimore: Penguin Books, 1967)

[11] Ada Louise Huxtable, "Modern-Life Battle: Conquering Clutter" in *The Riverside Reader*, second edition (Boston: Houghton Mifflin, 1985)

[12] Huxtable, op. cit. (same work as above)

[13] Irma Velasquez, from an unpublished manuscript called "Tortillas"

[14] William Brashler, "The Black Middle Class: Making It," *New York Times Magazine*, December 3, 1978

[15] Tom Wolfe, *The Right Stuff* (New York: Farrar, Straus & Giroux, 1979)

[16] Aesop, "The Frogs Desiring a King." Version by Meredith Sue Willis, based on the translation in *The Norton Reader*, edited by Arthur Eastman (New York: Norton, 1984)

[17] Linda Brent, "Incidents in the Life of a Slave Girl" in *The Classic Slave Narratives*, edited by Henry Louis Gates, Jr. (New York: New American Library, 1987)

[18] Georgia O'Keeffe, *Georgia O'Keeffe* (New York: Viking, 1976)

[19] From a report on a free school in New York's Lower East Side. I have long lost the name of the teacher, and the student's name has been changed.

[20] Leo Tolstoy, *Sebastopol Sketches* (New York: Penguin, 1986)

[21] Dashiell Hammett, *The Maltese Falcon* in *The Novels of Dashiell Hammett* (New York: Knopf, 1965)

BIBLIOGRAPHY

For More Writing Ideas

If you want more ideas for writing, read the following books:

• **Personal Fiction Writing** by Meredith Sue Willis. New York: Teachers & Writers Collaborative, 1984

• **Teaching and Writing Popular Fiction** by Karen Hubert. New York: Teachers & Writers Collaborative, 1976

The Young Writer's Handbook by Susan and Stephen Tchudi. New York: Scribner's, 1985

• **The Whole Word Catalogue 1**, edited by Rosellen Brown and others. New York: Teachers & Writers Collaborative, 1972

• **The Whole Word Catalogue 2**, edited by Bill Zavatsky and Ron Padgett. New York: McGraw-Hill/Teachers & Writers Collaborative, 1977

• **The Writing Workshop: Volumes 1 & 2** by Alan Ziegler. New York: Teachers & Writers Collaborative, 1981

Writing Your Way by Peter Stillman. Portsmouth, NH: Heinemann/Boynton Cook, 1984

- **Like It Was: A Complete Guide to Writing Oral History** by Cynthia Stokes Brown. New York: Teachers & Writers Collaborative, 1988

The Writer's Resource: Readings for Composition edited by Susan Day and Elizabeth McMahan. New York: McGraw-Hill, 1988.

To find these books, ask at your school or public library. If your library doesn't have the book you want, see if the librarian can get it for you from another library.

If you want to buy any of these books, see if your local bookstore can order them. The titles with the • symbol next to them can be ordered from Teachers & Writers Collaborative at the address given on the copyright page of this book.